EMMERDALE FAMILY ALBUM

A VILLAGE PORTRAIT

EMMERDALE FAMILY ALBUM
Michael Heatley

A VILLAGE PORTRAIT

YORKSHIRE
TELEVISION

BOXTREE

First published in Great Britain in 1994 by Boxtree Limited

Text © Michael Heatley/Yorkshire Television 1994
Photographs © Yorkshire Television 1994

Designed by Julian Holland
Printed and bound in Portugal by Printer Portuguesa for

Boxtree Limited
Broadwall House
21 Broadwall
London   SE1 9PL

A CIP catalogue entry for this book is available from the British
Library.

ISBN   1 85283 922 8

Jacket photographs courtesy of Yorkshire Television

Acknowledgements

Many thanks go to the actors of *Emmerdale*, both past and present, whom I've interviewed in the last two years. All have helped flesh out their characters, but thanks especially to Brendan Price with his useful background information on the McAllisters. Thanks also to John Barraclough and Bill Hill at the *Emmerdale* magazine, and John Stagg, Emily and the press team at Farsley. I'm grateful to editor Katy Carrington for her gentle persuasion when things needed to be done and weren't. Last, but certainly not least, thanks to my wife Chris for sitting patiently through many hundreds of episodes!

Dedicated to my Ma and Pa, Sheila and David.

Michael Heatley, 1994

The publishers would like to thank Andrea Pitchforth and Sheila Fitzhugh of the stills department of Yorkshire Television for their tireless research of the pictures used in the *Emmerdale Family Album* and the Farsley press office; also the Southwark Local Studies Library, London Borough of Southwark, and the Office of Population Censuses & Surveys for their advice and help with source material.

Contents

Introduction

NESTLED DEEP in the Yorkshire Dales, Emmerdale (previously known as Beckindale) has known human habitation for many centuries, Bronze age artefacts and Roman remains having been excavated from the surrounding countryside. Yet it is the families who have inhabited this supposedly sleepy village who have brought it to vibrant life. Whether meeting in church, at the local pub, playing the annually-contested cricket match with neighbouring Robblesfield (established in 1903), or combating the disastrous effects of the air crash of Christmas 1993, they have interacted, intermarried, fallen in and fallen out – often to dramatic effect.

Whether long-standing residents like the Sugdens at Emmerdale Farm or relative newcomers like the Tates at Home Farm, squires of the neighbourhood or tenant farmers scratching a living, each family has had its part to play in making history. This is a record not only of their lives but the traditional events that form the social calendar of the village community.

Opposite *In so many ways a typically uneventful Dales village, Beckindale hit the headlines in late 1993 as the site of an air crash. The residents voted to rename the village Emmerdale the following year, in an attempt to change its luck for the better.*

Beginnings and Traditions

*T*HE COUNTRY traditions that are so important to villages like Emmerdale follow the rhythm of the seasons. This is, of course, most pronounced on the farms of the area where lambing dominates spring and the harvest the autumn, then the winter comes and the cycle starts again.

Although local matters and customs have always predominated in the social calendar, one-off events like the Queen's Silver Jubilee in 1977 represent a chance for the village to put on their party hats and push the boat out. 'What a spread we put on *that* day,' Annie still recalls. But she can also remember

Right *Joint president of Beckindale Allotments Association, Seth Armstrong has always been keen to become involved in local competitions – though competition from Amos and, more recently, Nick Bates has kept him on his toes. He is pictured here at the 1985 Harvest Festival.*

Opposite *Beckindale celebrated the Queen's Silver Jubilee 1977, along with countless communities nationwide. And as with so many of the village's events in past years, the Sugdens are very much in the forefront of the picture.*

The Demdale Hunt remains an important part of local tradition, although the anti-bloodsports lobby and influx of outsiders has led to its continuation being questioned. Frank Tate, for instance, is ambivalent, though another Eighties arrival, Woolpack landlord Alan Turner, has enjoyed riding to hounds and still entertains the Hunt.

the VE Day celebrations when the flags were hung out to celebrate victory over Hitler's Germany. There was also sadness then, of course, for the men of the area who had exchanged pitchforks for rifles and ploughshares for bayonets, only to pay the ultimate price.

Christmas, Easter and the usual religious festivals are celebrated as they are everywhere else, the church and the public houses representing the usual venues for festivity. At the Woolpack in 1992, Alan Turner reinstated a custom of supplying free Christmas dinners for the village's senior citizens… only to discover that Ernie Shuttleworth at the Malt

Shovel, the Woolpack's rival hostelry, had done likewise and the pensioners intended to take advantage of both!

The Demdale Hunt is another organization that thrives on continuity and custom. Home Farm is the traditional venue for the Hunt Ball in March although present incumbent Frank Tate is no great lover of blood sports – especially since the Master of Foxhounds gave chase to his wife! The Boxing Day Hunt, with the traditional stirrup cup and other attendant ceremony, nonetheless remains an important part of the calendar.

In the summer, the annual cricket match against neighbouring Robblesfield always attracts interest. The fixture, with a history that dated back to 1903, is played not only for local pride, but with the Butterworth Bowl at stake. The annual church fête remains a significant social event, while Guy Fawkes' Night is celebrated in November by the village bonfire. In 1980, it was combined with the grandly titled Village Allotments Ball, while in 1989 Alan Turner's suit somehow found its way on to the guy!

Local cricket rivalries have always brought Beckindale's men together. Jack Sugden leads the applause as umpire Amos prepares to raise his finger.

CHALLENGE CRICKET MATCH

Beckindale vs. Emmerdale

THE PARISH COUNCIL INVITE YOUNG MEN FROM THE AGE OF 16 YEARS TO REPRESENT THE VILLAGE IN A CHALLENGE MATCH AGAINST ROBBLESFIELD ON SATURDAY 16TH JUNE, 1903.

ALL THOSE DESIROUS OF PLAYING MUST ASSEMBLE AT VERNEY'S FIELD AT 10.30 AM, IN THE CORRECT ATTIRE (WHITE SHIRT, WHITE FLANNELS, CAP). A LIGHT LUNCHEON AND TEA WILL BE PROVIDED.

SPECTATORS ARE ALSO WELCOME, IF OF A CALM AND GENTLE DISPOSITION. NO DOGS.

By order H. Butterworth

Hardest-fought of the inter-village cricket matches has traditionally been the annual Butterworth Bowl fixture with Robblesfield. An advert for the first such game went up around the area in 1903.

Christmas means both the vicar's bazaar and a pantomime. Amos Brearly's less than seasonal *Dracula* in early 1990 (written as a thriller but played, to Amos's bemusement, as a comedy) is well remembered, especially for Kathy Merrick finding Seth Armstrong unconscious in the coffin. Village plays are sometimes staged at other times of the year, and the late-Eighties production of *Toad Of Toad Hall* brought together the talents of Messrs Hinton (Ratty), Brearly (Toad) and Turner (Mole)!

But most of the traditions are based around the pagan rites of giving thanks for the harvest. The Seedcut is a major ritual, not to mention a fertility rite, and one that traditionally takes place on the farm that is last to gather in their harvest. A small corner of the last field is left uncut for the spirit of the harvest to retreat into. The previous year's Seed King presents each village lad with an ear of corn from the last sheaf, and the one with the most seeds is chased to the village hall where all the unwed girls are waiting, having elected a Seedcut Queen. If the boy can reach her – and a strategic window is usually left open! – he becomes the Seed King.

In Annie Sugden's youth, when she was still Annie Pearson, the Harvest Supper was held in a barn, but these days the village hall is generally considered warmer and more convenient. It's still decorated with lanterns and bales of straw, 'only somehow the atmosphere isn't the same. I shouldn't quibble, really: the important thing is that our village keeps up tradition.' That tradition has also included a barrel of ale from the squire, though would-be teetotaller Frank Tate may well argue that this has run its course.

The Harvest Supper is the farmers' way of thanking the labourers for their efforts – and suitably, since the singing and dancing invariably continues until the early hours, the labourers are always granted the next day off to attend to their hangovers!

Later in the year comes the Beckstone Thrash, another pagan ritual with a centuries-old history, connected with the beating of the bounds. The veterans of the village march around the parish boundary carrying candles and wooden staffs which they tap on the ground to 'thrash out' all the evil spirits from the parish for another year. The leader's staff is passed down from one to another as the young boys of the village follow awe-struck behind the procession.

Annie Sugden turns stallholder as the village lays on a Seventies fête, a certain way of boosting church funds in the pre-car boot sale age.

15

The elder statesmen of Beckindale process round the district in the Beating of the Bounds in 1974. Such old pagan festivals, designed to expel evil spirits, may not survive into another century.

Sam Pearson proudly held that staff for many years. His death in 1984 weakened the village's link with the past, while the greater number of 'incomers' in recent years has inevitably diluted the customs of yesteryear. Even so, it seems certain that at least some of the old traditions will survive into another century.

The undisguised fertility rite of the Seedcut is connected with the harvest and has its roots in ancient times, as this engraving, done by a local artist in the late 1700s, shows. These days, it is held in the village hall rather than a draughty barn.

The Old Families

THE VERNEYS

FOR THE OLDER inhabitants of Emmerdale, Home Farm – the old manor house just outside the village – represented the traditional way of country life. It was the home of the squire who, since time immemorial, had presided benevolently over his tenant farmers from the big house. He'd contribute a barrel of ale on village feast days and generally keep a paternal eye on the community.

The Verney family had long been top dogs of the village, and George Verney, who died in 1978, was the last of a long line. He'd married a woman rather younger than himself, and in 1973 been obliged to administer a public horsewhipping to Jack when he sought to bring a little 'light' into her life. It was an

Now known as Home Farm, the imposing manor house just outside Beckindale was for many years the seat of the Verney family as Creskeld Hall. The family were local landowners from whom the farmers leased their smallholdings.

Dated 20th August 1931

Miffield Estate
(on behalf of George
Verney Esquire)

— to —

Mr Jacob Sugden

Freehold of Emmerdale
Farm and Premises as
stipulated under the conditions
of this document in the Parish
of Skipdale, Hotten in the
county of West Yorkshire

Clear Sale £750

George Verney

PRIVATE SALE

Left *Deeds to the Sugden's farm bought from the Miffield Estate. Sixty years later it was to be condemned as structurally unsound.*

Above *George Verney, the last in a long line of squires, died in 1978, leaving his estate to his nephew, Gerald.*

ironic clash of the district's two longest-standing families: only the Verneys could boast a longer traceable history than the Sugdens (and Sam Pearson, for one, would argue that point!).

On George's demise in Cannes, France, where he'd lived since the break-up of his marriage, the estate was inherited by his nephew Gerald Verney.

George Verney's nephew Gerald and his wife, Charlotte, were forced to sell the whole estate after George's death in France.

He was no squire-in-waiting but a small-time London businessman; the colossal death duties he faced left him and his wife Charlotte no option but to sell. Old George had on a number of occasions considered the option of selling the buildings for use as a college, but this time it was the whole estate – lock, stock and barrel.

And that had possible wide-ranging repercussions throughout the community. The freehold of Emmerdale Farm itself had been bought from the Miffield Estate which the Verneys administered, but much still remained in their hands: many shops in the village were rented from them, as was the recreation ground by the parish council. That raised the spectre, as Sam Pearson said, of 'bungalows going up on the cricket pitch'. But as Annie sensibly observed, 'It's no good harking back to the good old days when the folk at the Hall felt a responsibility for Beckindale in general.'

The sale brought a territorial dispute in its wake in the shape of a 20-acre field claimed by Emmerdale Farm and the estate agents handling the sale which, it turned out, had been rented from George Verney by Jacob Sugden for a bottle of whisky a year! Jack Sugden paid rather more for the old mill at Connelton which was originally built by a member of the Verney family in the nineteenth century. (Demdyke Row was built by the Verneys for the men who worked there.) The mill was later converted into cottages.

The eventual purchasers of what had traditionally been known as 'Verney's' were NY Estates, and the changes were rung with a vengeance at the newly renamed Home Farm. The squire had traditionally turned a blind eye to a spot of poaching, but now Seth Armstrong – the neighbourhood's most notorious poacher – was appointed as gamekeeper.

An amusing postscript occurred in 1991, when Turner and Wilks read Amos Brearly's diaries and discovered that Seth Armstrong was, in fact, an illegitimate descendant of the Verney family. But any possible claims to ownership of Home Farm had been obscured by NY's purchase and subsequent disposal of the property to Frank Tate – his current boss!

THE GIMBELS

The Gimbels lived at Holly Farm, adjoining
Emmerdale Farm, a smallholding originally tenanted
in the last century by a recluse who patrolled its
boundaries with a gun and a dog. If Jim Gimbel was
distinctly anti-social, he was not quite as bad as his
predecessor: his wife Freda and Annie Sugden were
firm friends who belonged to the local Women's
Institute and regularly went to the market in Hotten
together.

Jim and Freda Gimbel had three children: Kathy
was the eldest, with Martin, next and Davy six years
younger. Jim Gimbel had always been distinctly old-
fashioned, so it was no surprise that, when Kathy
discovered she was pregnant by boyfriend Terry
Davis, the couple had been told in no uncertain
terms to do the decent thing and marry. Her return
to Holly Farm after she lost the child ended the
marriage, to a man everyone in the village knew as a
'bad lot'.

She had much in common with Joe Sugden, the
handsome young farmer from over the way. Both
were former schoolfriends who had married in haste
and were now repenting at leisure, so it was not
surprising when in 1977 the pair moved in together
at 3 Demdyke Row despite a tide of neighbourhood
disapproval. To make matters more complex still,
Martin had started dating Rosemary Kendall, the
teenage daughter of Annie's cousin, who was staying
at Emmerdale Farm while her mother was in hospital.

Martin was distinctly unhappy at home, because
at the age of 20 his father still expected him to work
for pocket-money. He'd left home once before, but
departed for good after one final argument with his

*Pious and strait-laced farmer Jim Gimbel alienated his
family and eventually chose a suicide solution.*

Left *Kathy Gimbel incurred her father's wrath for living with another married person, Joe Sugden.*

Above *Forced to choose between her husband and children, Freda Gimbel eventually quit Holly Farm.*

overbearing father, enlisting in the Army. Wife Freda followed the example of her children and walked out on Jim after he raised his hand to Davy. Abandoned by his nearest and dearest, Jim chose to end it all, by means of a shotgun.

The postman noticed that the cattle hadn't been milked, and informed Joe: the police discovered the body too late to save Jim Gimbel, who died of self-inflicted wounds. Rightly or wrongly, Kathy held herself responsible, a fact that also spelled the death knell for her relationship with Joe. At Holly Farm a young couple, Winn and Nicky Groves, moved in to take the Gimbels' place on a farm that had passed, via Messrs Turner and Joe Sugden, into NY Estates' ownership.

THE LONGTHORNS

Like the Tollys and the Gimbels, to name but two, the Longthorn family were typical tenant farmers of Beckindale, running their business on leasehold terms under the tolerant eye of the Verneys. Clifford was stolid and hardworking, while his wife was a pillar of the local community who, along with churchwarden Annie Sugden, was instrumental in holding charity events for the church restoration purposes. The Longthorns had two children, but it was the studious, bespectacled Andy, a sixth former at Hotten Comprehensive, who was to blot his copybook in 1983.

Plied with sherry at the vicarage, where brother Jackie was temporarily lodging after setting light to his caravan, Sandie Merrick had later allowed boyfriend Andy to make love to her for the first and last time. Discovering she was pregnant, she confided in Jackie who, with typical hot-headedness, marched

Andy Longthorn (right) *in conversation with friend Jackie Merrick, the brother of his girlfriend, Sandie. When news of their unplanned child leaked out, Andy and Jackie came to blows.*

up to Lower Hall Farm and blacked Andy's eye.

An unsuspecting Clifford Longthorn demanded retribution for this seemingly unprovoked attack which, into the bargain, had broken his son's spectacles. When the truth emerged, Clifford played a different tune. He brought a contrite Andy to Emmerdale Farm to announce that his son would marry Sandie, give up his studies and take over the farm when he came of age.

Sandie had other ideas: she decided to have the baby – a daughter named Louise – and give her up for adoption. Andy left the area for university as scheduled, while the Longthorns left their farm in 1986, after being evicted by NY Estates, and moved to Lincoln.

One year later, 30 acres of Lower Hall Farm land adjoining Home Farm and Emmerdale was put up for auction. With Jack Sugden and Harry Mowlam bidding the price up, the land sold for a record £1,600 per acre.

THE TOLLYS

The Tollys were long-established Emmerdale tenant farmers, the union of the notoriously cantankerous Enoch and his long-suffering wife Grace having been blessed with two daughters, Naomi and Hannah. Their relatively uneventful life ebbed and flowed with the seasons, but was cruelly turned upside down in 1981 when Enoch lost his life in a freak tractor accident. Grace was understandably distraught at this turn of events, but help was at hand in the unlikely yet undoubtedly kind-hearted form of Home Farm gamekeeper Seth Armstrong.

Enoch Tolly peruses the Good Book. His accidental death in 1981 found his wife in desperate straits.

It was he who persuaded her to employ Daniel Hawkins, who had until recently been a fellow employee of NY Estates, to make up the numbers – an arrangement that suited both parties admirably. Unfortunately, even with outside assistance, Grace and her daughters proved unequal to the struggle of keeping the smallholding going in the face of unfavourable economic conditions, and the family was finally forced to sell up in the following year.

The farm's head lease, previously held by the Verney family, had passed to NY Estates when Home Farm was sold. Alan Turner, whom NY Estates appointed as manager in residence at Home Farm, took possession and attempted to use the Tolley farmhouse to persuade Matt Skilbeck to leave Emmerdale Farm and join him. Matt declined: Daniel Hawkins, however, swallowed his pride and returned to the NY payroll.

Grace Tolly with one of her daughters, Hannah. Sadly, neither could save their livelihood after Enoch's passing.

The Clergy

The Skipdale Chronicle

21st JUNE 1882   ESTABLISHED 1850

ST MARY'S ABLAZE
FOUL PLAY SUSPECTED

A FIRE that severely damaged Beckindale's Parish Church of St Mary in the early hours of Thursday morning is today being investigated by the Hotten constabulary. They are seeking a young man of about

Vicar of St Mary's, the Reverend Thomas Holt, was too distressed to comment, but choirmaster Sam Anderson told our Beckindale Reporter: "I don't want to say it was young Charles's fault, but he

thirteen years, seen fleeing from the scene on foot. He answers the description of Charles Maudsley who, on the previous evening, was expelled from the church choir for smoking in the vestry.

has the cheek of the devil and they say there is no smoke without fire."

Fortunately, the vestry's much-admired stained-glass window survived the blaze.

THE VILLAGE has had a parish church since AD989. Then, as now, St Mary's Church was one of the village's social centres, where people would not only worship but mix at christenings, weddings and funerals. Part of the current church is of Norman origin, though the rest is Victorian Gothic, added after the disastrous fire of 1882, believed locally to be the work of a disgruntled choirboy! The vestry contains a treasured piece of Italian stained glass. The vicarage is a fine old Georgian manse with splendidly large and well-proportioned rooms.

The Reverend **Edward Ruskin** was the incumbent at St Mary's in the early Seventies, and presided at a time of deep sadness for the Sugdens.

Left *How the local paper of the time saw the St Mary's church fire of 1882.*

Below *A view of the church, unchanged for over a century now.*

Far Left *William Hockley came to St Mary's from Africa, but didn't stay long.*

Left *The Rev. Edward Ruskin and his wife, Liz, made Beckindale their home in the early Seventies.*

In the space of a couple of years he buried not only Jacob, Annie's husband, but her daughter Peggy and grandchildren Sam and Sally.

Ex-missionary **William Hockley** became the next vicar in 1977, and was often to be seen about the village on his bicycle – a habit he may perhaps have picked up in Africa, his last port of call while spreading the Christian gospel. The Reverend **David Cowper** succeeded him later that same year, but his stay was also to be a brief one. Stability returned to the parish of Emmerdale and Demdale with the appointment of **Donald Hinton**, who served from 1977 to 1989.

Far Left *David Cowper – a short-lived 1977 appointment to the Beckindale parish.*

Right The Rev. Donald Hinton pictured in pensive mood, with troublesome son, Clive.

The Vicarage provided lodgings for many souls over the years: Dolly Acaster, when she was turned out of the Woolpack by Amos, Pat Harker, and later, at the request of the police, her arsonist son Jackie. The position of parish priest in Emmerdale is just as important to the community as the Woolpack landlord. Indeed, and Hinton was not averse to visiting the hostelry as part of his pastoral duties!

Donald Hinton's infrequent absences were covered by the Reverend **Bob Jerome** or,

Although much appreciated by his parishioners, he enjoyed uneasy relationships with both son Clive (who, after visiting his father in 1978, was arrested in Athens for gun-running), and daughter Barbara who, having left her husband Brian in London in 1983, took a job as Alan Turner's secretary at NY Estates. She was more or less pushed into a relationship with Joe Sugden after her father, who'd disclosed her whereabouts to Brian, turned her out when no reconciliation was forthcoming.

As churchwarden Annie was not best pleased, and in the end Joe was offered a welcome escape route from the gossip-mongers with promotion to a position in France; Barbara declined to go with him. Instead she returned to London to start a new life in 1983, sparing her father's feelings by saying she'd gone back to Brian.

Far Right *Bob Jerome was sometimes seen at St Mary's as Donald Hinton's deputy.*

occasionally, by the returning **Edward Ruskin**. The Reverend **Bill Jeffries** was appointed as assistant minister in 1982, but differences of opinion ensured his stay was a short one. Though Hinton became rural dean that year, he refused an appointment as Archdeacon, seeing it as a political appointment that would take him away from his parishioners.

In 1986 came excitement when Hinton was briefly held hostage at gunpoint by Derek Warner, an associate of pig farmer Harry Mowlam, after it was discovered the two had fallen out over the proceeds from an armed robbery. Mowlam was murdered, but happily Hinton escaped unharmed. In quieter moments, he took solace in his collection of books and butterflies.

The marriage of Joe Sugden and Kate Hughes in April 1989 was to be one of Donald Hinton's last official duties before he retired to Coventry that

August. He returned in late 1993 for the marriage of Annie Sugden and Leonard Kempinski, attending as a guest but forced to officiate when the presiding minister contracted laryngitis.

Since Hinton's departure, **Tony Charlton** has been his only permanent replacement. He made his first appearance in August 1990 when he entered the Woolpack to use the telephone after discovering he'd lost his new house keys! A modern churchman, he was often seen without his dog-collar and was very interested in the young folk of Emmerdale.

Before entering the church, Tony Charlton had taught English Literature at a High School in Dalston, London, and was a voluntary worker at an inner-city youth centre. He started a three-year theology course and was ordained in June 1990. Tony's first post as curate was with Hotten Parish Council, who leased

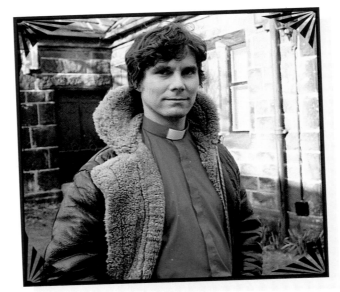

Far left *Tony Charlton was undoubtedly Beckindale's dishiest vicar, but fell for the unavailable Kathy Merrick.*

Left *Bill Jeffries' laid-back style was one which his senior minister, Rev. Hinton, found difficult to accommodate and resulted in the former's swift departure from the parish.*

him the small cottage where he lived.

Sadly, one of his first duties in August 1990 was to bury Pete Whiteley. Having visited Kate Sugden (the driver who hit Whiteley) in prison, he later attempted to involve her in church affairs. He would be unsuccessful in this, but after falling in love with Kathy Merrick, Charlton left for London, realizing there was no future in the romance.

28th April 1983   **HOTTEN COURIER**   **Features**

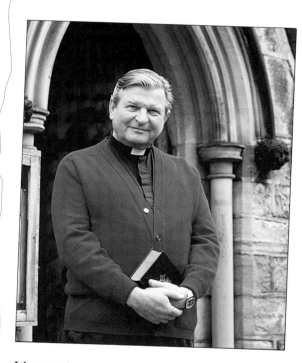

It's now six years since I was asked whether I would like to move to Beckindale: at the time I was unsure whether I would enjoy the peace and stability of a small village parish after the hurly-burly of the city. I imagined that I would no longer be involved in issues of great importance, but how wrong I was.

In a thriving community like Beckindale life is never dull. I have found myself involved in a wide variety of activities very different perhaps from those affecting an urban priest. When I was studying at theological college nobody warned me that part of my function as a parson would be to organize dog races, horticultural shows or lead the parish's bid to win the best kept village in the Dales competition! Equally, I had no idea of the passions and rivalry engendered on such occasions: it is very much a part of a vicar's duty to direct these strongly-felt passions along Christian paths and to represent the Christian ethic even to those who do not even nominally call themselves Christians.

The village of Emmerdale is one of the most beautiful in all the Dales and the Church of St Mary's is surely the jewel in its crown: but I am sad to report that the main roof of the Church has major structural problems which, according to our surveyors, will probably cost in the region of £5,000. It is a building in which all the village take pride and it's not just the worshippers who make use of it – almost all non-churchgoers still find themselves in church for christenings, weddings and funerals. I would like all the people of Beckindale to be aware of their responsibilities to our church in this our time of need.

Reverend Donald Hinton

Right *During the Eighties, Donald Hinton occasionally ventured into print in the pages of the* Hotten Courier.

The Woolpack

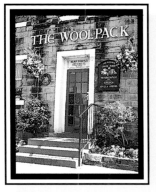

THE OLD Victorian hostelry was often patronized by one of the younger Verneys, a drunkard and a rake, during the Edwardian era. It was the scene of the village's greatest scandal when, after Verney boasted of seducing a local farmer's daughter, the farmer in question shot him. The current Woolpack, opened after the old one was declared structurally unsound in 1976, was built for a corn chandler and his family. The wine bar area was rebuilt after the 1993 plane crash, in the course of which historic human remains believed to be from the Viking era were discovered.

Above *Despite Alan Turner's modernization, the Woolpack in 1994 retained much of its olde-worlde charm.*

Left *The Woolpack in 1983, when Amos Brearly's name over the door was obscured by over-enthusiastic ivy!*

31

The Woolpack has always been Beckindale's premier public house. This earlier version of its pub sign, from the turn of the century, depicts the local origin of the name.

AMOS BREARLY

Born on All Fool's Day 1920, Amos Brearly came to the village as landlord of the Woolpack after the war, during which he served in Africa, Italy and France as a member of the Royal Artillery.

He ran his pub *his* way, refusing to bow to trends. Such 'innovations' as providing food for tourists were achieved with little grace, and he saw the opening of the taproom for youngsters as something of a social service to keep them out of trouble. Alan Turner, his successor as landlord, would turn it into a food-serving wine bar.

Amos's eccentricities have not always been in the best interests of the business. His determination to open and close exactly on time have often had Seth and his cronies hammering on the door, to no effect, demanding to be let in. He frowned upon his working customers taking too long a dinner break. Once, while experimenting with longer opening hours, he even tried to cut down the amount his customers drank!

Amos, descended from a long line of Bridlington undertakers, was something of a dead loss when it came to the female of the species. When his regulars told him the pub needed a woman's touch he proposed to Annie Sugden on this basis. Soon after, Dolly Acaster moved in as live-in barmaid, but Amos couldn't cope with living with a woman and she had to move out, although she stayed on as barmaid.

He never married, although he was once engaged to a lady named Gloria Pinfold, who jilted him for a pork butcher in Harrogate at a ball to celebrate VJ Day. He claims that she did it because of the rationing and he 'still can't look down at his sausage

Amos Brearly was a familiar sight behind the bar until his much-regretted retirement in 1991.

33

in a morning without feeling a pang of sorrow'.

Gloria resurfaced briefly in 1989, when a balloon flight prize at a local show landed Amos in Robin Hood's Bay. He disappeared for some days and returned to the pub with Gloria – who was on the make. Love soon turned to terror, and he was relieved when the same pork butcher, now with a string of shops to his name, whisked Gloria off to Paignton.

Aside from his licensee's duties, Amos was for many years a correspondent for the *Hotten Courier*, and spent hours crafting articles – usually to find them completely rewritten once they appeared in the paper. The job provided a useful cover for his natural nosiness.

Amos was asked to give Dolly away at her wedding to Matt and is godfather to Sam Skilbeck. An enthusiastic participant in village shows, choirs and the like, he was deeply disappointed to be left out of the church choir in 1988, especially as he often went about his work in the pub singing snatches from Gilbert and Sullivan. *Dracula*, which he wrote as a serious drama, was a huge comic success in January 1990.

In the summer of that year, he suffered a mild stroke during Annie's 70th birthday celebrations, the aftermath of which – a slight paralysis of his left-side – temporarily forced him to give up his duties.

His only family are his brother Ezra, with whom he has a relationship very much like that he has with Seth, Aunt Emily and cousin, Alice. They all live in Whitehaven, where Ezra is a butcher. In 1988, Ezra developed a temporary allergy to meat and descended on the Woolpack; his first act on entering the pub was to order a round for everyone 'on the

Amos Brearly pictured with his good friend and Woolpack co-owner, Henry Wilks, at a local fête back in 1974.

Amos's Aunt Emily, pictured with cousin Alice (right), *could always be relied upon to keep the publican in hand.*

house'. Despite his love-hate relationship with Ezra, Amos enjoyed Christmas 1989 with him and Aunt Emily, who treated the two elderly men as naughty little boys.

Amos never learned to drive and was dependent on Wilks to chauffeur him around. One occasion, when he discovered the taxi fare doubled at midnight, he insisted on being dropped three miles short of the village at a minute to midnight and walked home.

Although he never talks about money, Amos never seemed to spend it unnecessarily, and hence

was able to move to Spain in 1991 and enjoy a well-earned retirement in the sunshine. Annie was one of several welcome guests to make the journey from the village via Leeds/Bradford airport, and it was Amos who played Cupid and introduced her to retired Polish businessman Leonard Kempinski: the pair would marry in 1993.

Their relationship gave Amos all the excuse he needed to show his face in the Woolpack again, making many an observation on how standards had fallen under the current incumbent, Alan Turner.

HENRY WILKS

Henry Wilks and his good friend Amos served side by side for so many years behind the bar of the Woolpack that you could barely mention the name of one without the other. But when Bradford mill-owner Henry arrived in the village, having taken early retirement when his wife Maggie died, he was initially regarded with suspicion.

Within weeks of moving in at Inglebrook, a large house adjoining Emmerdale Farm land, their new neighbour was busy annoying the Sugdens by re-establishing long-forgotten rights of way. When he purchased the freehold of Emmerdale Farm from under their noses, he became the Sugdens' landlord.

Yet his proposal to turn the farm into a company, and provide the capital for much-needed new machinery, eased Annie's financial worries and provided her with a trusted friend. There was nearly more than friendship involved, since Henry unsuccessfully proposed to her on at least one occasion.

As the farm episode proved, Henry had clearly not hung up his head for commerce with his business suit. Fortunately, he was on hand to secure the future of another village institution – the Woolpack.

It had been his intention to settle with daughter Marian at Inglebrook, but it was not to be: an accidental fire destroyed his dream home, while

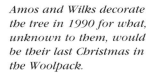

Amos and Wilks decorate the tree in 1990 for what, unknown to them, would be their last Christmas in the Woolpack.

Marian emigrated to New Zealand after her romance with Jack Sugden failed. (She would eventually settle in Italy with husband Paolo Rossetti, and bear Henry a grandchild.)

Initially, he rented a room at the Woolpack from Amos, but when the brewery put the pub up for sale, Henry was on hand to provide financial backing. A pub was an unlikely residence for someone of Henry's wealth, but as a naturally outgoing person with no family to hand he found the life congenial.

His company wasn't always appreciated by Amos, at least not on the face of it. Any 'improvements' mooted for the pub – from spicy sausages to microwaves and computerised tills – were always debated down to the last detail, and often in public! But when the chips were down, the two would be there shoulder-to-shoulder, and when Amos was laid low by a stroke in 1990 it was Henry who pushed him all the way along the road to recovery.

When the old Woolpack's foundations crumbled in 1976 and a move was proposed, Amos was concerned about a local legend that the new site, formerly a corn chandler's residence, was haunted. Despite his partner's doubts, Henry proceeded with what he considered a wise investment and the new Woolpack soon replaced its predecessor as a cornerstone of the community.

Henry was very much at home out of doors. He was a keen ornithologist and conservationist, and once saved a family of Peregrine falcons on Keller Fell from extinction at the hands of egg thieves. A loyal servant of his adopted village, he served as both churchwarden and parish councillor, and when not 'on duty' acted in many stage plays in the church hall. One year he appeared in drag, which raised a few eyebrows, but unlike Amos, Henry was never afraid to laugh at himself.

Over nearly two decades until his fatal heart attack in 1991, Henry Wilks played a major part in keeping the fabric of this farming community together – firstly by bringing an industrialist's vision to the running of the farm when its future seemed in doubt, then assuring that the Woolpack remained in local hands.

Henry's daughter, Marian, whose on-off affair with Jack Sugden brought her father many a grey hair.

The Sugdens

THE EMMERDALE farmhouse, home of the Sugdens for many a decade, has seen family members come and go. In 1993 the decision was taken by Jack to move to Hawthorn Cottage, where Joe and his first wife Christine had briefly made their home almost two decades earlier. Emmerdale had been found to be structurally unsound, old lead mine workings underneath the area having opened up and swallowed Jack's tractor. So a long-established chapter of Sugden history closed as another opened.

When subsidence struck, Hawthorn Cottage was selected in 1993 as the new Emmerdale Farm.

ANNIE SUGDEN

When Annie Pearson married Jacob Sugden at the age of 25 in 1945 and came to live at Emmerdale with him and his father, she little knew that half a century later she would remain the village's elder statesperson and the matriarch of a family that had continued to flourish thanks to her surviving children Jack and Joe. (A third, Peggy, had died in 1973.)

Jacob had been a drinker, and it was left to Annie and her children to do most of the farming even when he was alive. A staunch believer in the family, she always defended her offspring to the hilt against

Joe, Matt and Peggy Skilbeck, Jack, Annie and Sam Pearson pictured at Jacob's funeral, 1972.

CERTIFICATE OF DEATH

DEATH	Entry Number **446**

Registration District Sub-district	**HOTTEN**	Administrative area *West Yorkshire*

1. Date and place of death	*10th October 1972 General Hospital, Hotten*

2. Name and surname	3. Sex *Male*
Jacob Joseph Sugden	4. Maiden surname of woman who has married —

5. Date and place of birth	*5th May 1910 Beckindale, Yorks*

6. Occupation and usual address	*Farmer, Emmerdale Farm Beckindale, Yorks*

7. (a) Name and surname of informant *Registrar General Hospital, Hotten, Yorks*	(b) Qualification —
(c) Usual address	

8. Cause of death
Liver failure

9. I certify that the particulars given by me above are true to the best of my knowledge and belief.	Signature of informant

10. Date of registration *17 October, 1972*	11. Signature of registrar *James W. Barnett*

Jacob Sugden's death in 1972 closed a chapter in the family's history – but an unwilling Jack did not wish to take on his father's mantle.

outsiders, despite all the problems they have caused her, choosing to deliver her criticism in private.

Because of her policy of keeping the family together, Annie has constantly acted as referee between Joe and Jack. She has often appeared to favour Joe, however, despairing of Jack's whimsical nature. Known to Jack and Joe as 'Ma', and to Sarah and Rachel as 'Annie', her background has led her to approve of the various Emmerdale wives supporting their husbands as she had, and being involved with the farm.

Over the years, Annie has had numerous marriage proposals. One or two have come from old boyfriends, who have materialized and then disappeared. One came from Amos Brearly, who believed that the Woolpack needed a woman's touch. He advertised for a barmaid when rejected!

Annie's most persistent suitor was Henry Wilks. The two started as enemies when Wilks moved into Inglebrook – a house doomed, like Crossgill, to burn

The Skilbeck twins are christened in 1973, but neither they nor their mother Peggy (right) *would survive to enjoy continued happiness.*

down. After the fire, Wilks moved into Emmerdale for a short period before going to the Woolpack. He and Annie became friends, he proposed to her and she turned him down. Then, in 1989, he was planning to propose to her again – but, by mutual agreement, he didn't ask and she didn't turn him down!

Annie is a regular churchgoer and has been a churchwarden at St Mary's since 1975. Despite her relatively advanced age, she passed her driving test in 1975 after losing her lift to Hotten Market during a dispute with the neighbouring Gimbels. She wears glasses for reading and sewing, and is still mobile despite two 'plastic' knees: indeed, she went dancing with Eddie Hammond, Kate's father, when he stayed at the farm in 1989.

She was a leading light in the Women's Institute and Mother's Union, and enjoys the theatre (but not Shakespeare) when the occasion presents itself. Annie rarely goes to the Woolpack for a drink, preferring to entertain guests, although she has been known to drink the occasional sherry.

Annie announced her retirement from family farming activities in July 1990, feeling she was too old to be out in the fields. At the farm, she used to look after the poultry before Kate took over. She also ran the farm shop (with Dolly and Kate) in 1988-89, and had a bell fitted in the yard for customers to ring, though the shop fell into disuse after Dolly left and Kate was jailed.

Annie was almost killed in 1988 in the fire at Crossgill. Builder Phil Pearce, whose carelessness caused the fire, saved her. Yet tragedy, so narrowly avoided on that occasion, would revisit her life five years later after a late-flowering romance had seemed to give her even more to live for.

On a visit to Amos Brearly in his Spanish retirement home, she met retired Polish businessman Leonard Kempinski. The understandable protectiveness of the Sugden sons made life uncomfortable at first. Only when Leonard revealed the extent of his personal wealth were they convinced that he was not a gold-digger, hoping to dupe them out of their inheritance.

Further trouble ensued when Annie learned on her unscheduled return from Spain that Emmerdale had been condemned as structurally unsound. She declined to take up residence at Hawthorn Cottage (later renamed Emmerdale, at Amos's suggestion) and moved to Mill Cottage with Kathy and Chris while family relations were re-established. Life did get back to normal, despite a cake cooked by Sarah with pheasant eggs that, unknown to her, Seth had injected with mustard to deter (feathered) thieves!

Annie and Leonard decided to cement their

Annie Sugden becomes Mrs Leonard Kempinski, in the company of Rev. Donald Hinton (left) and Amos (right).

The inimitable Sam Pearson profers a pike for inspection. Many old traditions died with him in November 1985.

SAM PEARSON

Annie Sugden's father Sam Pearson represented the farm's link with the old days and old ways, and his passing in 1985 truly marked the end of an era.

Sam had served at Flanders during World War One. He later returned to the land and by the time he retired was farm manager at Verney's, moving to Emmerdale when his daughter married farmer Jacob Sugden. When Sam was made a partner in the new Emmerdale company after Jacob's death, he decided he didn't want the responsibility and sold his share to Wilks for £500, using the proceeds to train dogs.

Though generally opposed to change – using the phone was one pet hate – Sam nevertheless got on with young people. Those who came under the farmhouse roof, like Rosemary, daughter of Annie's cousin Jean Kendall, and Jack's stepdaughter-to-be Sandie Merrick, he treated as surrogate grandchildren. Yet the genuine articles upset him with their disregard for morality – Joe living out of wedlock with Kathy Gimbel and Jack's courting of the separated Pat Merrick.

After suffering a stroke in 1977, Sam holidayed in Rome with Annie, where they stayed with Jack. He agreed to return for a longer period – on his own this time – as Jack wanted to write his life story, grandly entitled *One Man In Time.*

Sam was always in the forefront of maintaining country traditions like the keenly-contested cricket fixtures with neighbouring villages. Despite his age, he was also on the committee of the bowls club and the horticulture society.

In his role as chairman of the Emmerdale cricket team, he was instrumental in returning the treasured Butterworth Bowl from the Woolpack, having replaced the stolen original with one of his own before locating the genuine ball with the help of

friendship by tying the knot: they were married at St Mary's on 28 October 1993 by the returning Reverend Donald Hinton. The pair then decided to buy a cottage and settle in the area.

But as Joe drove them to the airport *en route* to a Christmas in the sun, their car left the road when the ill-fated Eastern European plane descended on the village. Leonard died in the crash, while Annie spent the next three months in a coma, waking only when presented with her new grandchild Victoria. Initially, her memories of the recent past and her second husband were few, but it was clear there was much adjustment needed for Annie to come to terms with the terrible events.

Matt, Sam, Annie and Joe: a Pearson, a Skilbeck and two Sugdens – all vital to the running of Emmerdale Farm.

Annie and scout Billy Luttercombe before the deception was discovered.

Despite his age, Sam was no pushover, as local tearaways Steve Hawker and Pip Coulter found out in 1978 when they took him hostage at gunpoint after robbing the Woolpack. He survived the ordeal, but was to spend time in hospital when a growth was discovered in his throat. Though many feared the worst, including Sam himself, it turned out to be nothing more serious than a piece of almond!

Before his marriage, a youthful Sam had planned to ask Nellie Dawson to marry him. Years later, and now a widower, he realized he still had feelings for her and proposed in 1976 but she turned him down, saying they were both too set in their ways. Nevertheless, when NY Estates tried to force her out of her home, Sam was quick to lead the battle to save her cottage and show who Jack had inherited his stubborn streak from!

As the years passed, Sam took every opportunity to prove he could still teach the 'youngsters' a thing or two. He accompanied Seth into Verney's woods one night in 1978 to snare rabbits – but was caught red-handed with a sackful of pheasant by Trevor Thatcher of NY Estates, the new owners. Seth refused to own up, fearing he would be sent to prison, and both the accused were relieved when the matter was dropped.

A competition provided Sam and Annie with a cruise holiday when he won first prize with a slogan he'd borrowed from Jack. But he needed no help when it came to cultivation. For many years, Sam was in charge of the farm's kitchen garden, and his green fingers nurtured some prime produce.

While much lamented, the manner of Sam Pearson's passing in November 1985 was nothing less than appropriate. Having won first prize at the annual show with his pumpkin, he celebrated most royally. When daughter Annie brought in his morning cup of tea next day he had slipped away.

The death of Sam Pearson left not only an empty place at the farmhouse table but a gap in village society that would never be filled. His generation

Jack's best-selling novel, The Field Of Tares, *took him out of the Emmerdale orbit for many years.*

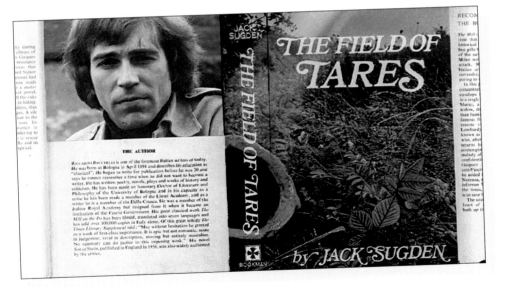

represented a last link with customs and practices like the Beckstone Thrash and beating the bounds (see page 15) which would thenceforth be one step nearer being consigned to the history books.

JACK SUGDEN

Over the years, Annie and Jacob Sugden's eldest child has so often turned out to be the black sheep of the family – yet in 1994, when his brother Joe left, he remained the sole inheritor of his father's mantle. That had seemed less than likely when he returned to Emmerdale for his father's funeral in 1972, having previously left for London after an argument over intensive farming, and found he had inherited the farm. He didn't want it, but was persuaded by Henry Wilks to set up a partnership with the rest of his family. Yet he was off again just a year later in pursuit of Wilks's daughter, Marian, who had gone to Italy.

At this time, Jack was a writer and had a successful novel, *The Field of Tares* (a story, based on personal experience, of a man being torn between two women) which he later turned into a screenplay at Cinecitta in Rome. Over the years, his writing – and the money he made from it – has been forgotten.

Jack had been teenage sweethearts with Pat Harker, but their romance ended when Jack moved to London. They married in October 1982, two years after she returned to the area, and had a son, Robert, in 1986, but Pat died in a car crash just five months later. Apart from Pat Harker, the other great love of Jack's life was Marian Wilks. Having chased her to Italy in 1973, their romance was rekindled years later in 1987, when Marian visited the village with her husband, Paolo, and their baby Niccolo. In the summer of 1988, when Marian's marriage to the wheelchair-bound Paolo was crumbling, she returned once more to the village and Jack again followed her back to Italy. After a further year of trying to persuade her to leave Paolo – with plenty of promises but no action – Jack gave up and came home.

On his return, Jack contacted Sarah Connolly, with whom he had had a brief relationship early in 1988. His feelings for Sarah were strong, but complicated by what was happening with Marian. Local gossips observed that Jack only returned to Sarah because things with Marian didn't work out, but Sarah was fully aware of the situation.

He moved into the Skilbecks' house after lodging with Kathy and persuaded Sarah to live with him – on a no-strings-attached basis – in January 1990. They even went to the length of drawing up a semi-serious contract to stipulate that they were sharing a house rather than living together! Their strange relationship was a puzzle to Annie, although no-one else seemed to comment about it.

Jack is everything his critics say – whimsical, bloody-minded, annoyingly facetious and totally unpredictable. He is also charming, principled and ready to fight anybody to defend his beliefs. He has an air of not taking things seriously, but this is deceptive, as he has proved himself capable of going to ridiculous lengths to prove a point.

His arrest while protesting against a planned nuclear dump on Pencross Fell in 1987 came after he stopped son Jackie getting arrested himself! In equally impetuous fashion, his response to Joe's felling of trees at Home Farm was to plant twenty acres of saplings at Emmerdale Farm, even though he would never live to see them mature nor would the

Robert James Sugden is christened, 1986, as parents Pat and (a somewhat reluctant) Jack pose for the family album.

farm gain anything from it. He hates the thought of the Dales being turned into 'a holiday playground', and has locked horns with Frank Tate whom he regards as the embodiment of this kind of attitude. Yet in 1994 he was not beyond asking Tate to help fund a new farm shop which, he argued, might benefit guests of the recently opened Holiday Village.

As a working farmer, the recession hit Jack hard. Once an idealist who saw Emmerdale as a way of life, not simply a business, Jack has been forced to adopt Joe's view that the family farm – and the way of life he loves – will only survive if it's run as a business.

Despite 'running away' in the past, the Nineties saw Jack firmly committed to Emmerdale – not least with a new mouth to feed in Victoria Anne.

SARAH CONNOLLY

Sarah Connolly first appeared in Emmerdale as a travelling librarian. Very much the professional single woman, she was determined to enjoy her free and easy lifestyle to the full with a host of friends of both sexes and a refusal to be tied down. It was this sparky independence that both attracted Jack Sugden and, when he couldn't change her, frustrated him! For her part, Sarah herself was confused by the attraction of Jack, who stood for a great many things she despised – commitment, exclusivity and a quiet domestic life surrounded by an extended family.

Local opinion claimed that Sarah's attitude was – at least partly – responsible for driving him back into the arms of his old flame Marian Wilks. Yet on his return from Italy in 1989 for Jackie's funeral, it was Sarah he sought as someone he could talk to rather

Sarah Connolly and Jack Sugden finally married in 1994 after many annual proposals had been rejected.

than stay with his family at the farm. She urged him to sort things out once and for all with Marian, which he did – and after Marian refused to come to England with him he returned alone.

Sarah, meanwhile, continued to lead her busy social life, but she and Jack gradually saw more and more of each other. Alarm bells rang when she insisted on going on her annual Christmas/New Year skiing holiday with a group of friends including Gerry, a casual boyfriend, but on her return Sarah surprised everybody – including, perhaps, herself – when she moved in with Jack.

At first she steadfastly clung on to her social life altogether – and equally steadfastly refused to have anything to do with the farm. She remained aloof from the Sugdens next door. She stopped Annie's habit of wandering in through the connecting door by simply nailing it up, declaring that she was used to living alone, not sharing a house with Jack and Robert, never mind Annie, Joe, Kate, Mark, Rachel and Lucy the dog!

The closure of the mobile library service in June 1990 represented a major threat to Sarah's independence. She was predictably annoyed when Jack went behind her back and offered her services to Amos and Wilks at the Woolpack, but at length accepted the part-time job with good grace and also agreed to help out on the farm when the Sugdens found themselves short-handed.

Drama struck after Chris and Kathy Tate's wedding in 1991 when Sarah was kidnapped by Jim Latimer, a recently released murderer with a grudge against Jack that dated back to the trial. He held her captive in a disused building, but she reacted with characteristic good sense and the situation was, happily, resolved peacefully.

Sarah involved herself in family matters with a will, tackling Mark about his shoplifting and

admitting that she had done the same herself as a teenager. She acquired local notoriety in early 1992 by hosting a 'raunchy underwear party' which attracted the men as eagerly as the ladies, while an outing to the dry ski slope at Skipdale that same year suggested she hadn't given up hope of changing her man – even though Jack outperformed her and she ended up twisting her ankle!

Jack and Sarah's relationship seemed as solid as most marriages, even though she declined his ritual proposals of marriage delivered each year on the anniversary of their meeting. Robert, Jack's child from his marriage to Pat, came to regard Sarah as

The arrival of baby Victoria Anne in early 1994 was the first bright spot after the plane crash weeks earlier.

Robert Sugden poses with Jack and Sarah at the gate of what is to become the new Emmerdale Farm.

age of 42. Soon after, they were brought even closer together when Victoria was taken seriously ill with a hole in her heart. Thankfully, after a long stay in Leeds hospital, she returned home, recovered.

ROBERT SUGDEN

Robert Sugden, Jack's son and heir, never knew his mother Pat, who died shortly after he was born. Robert's brother Jackie, born to Pat and Jack some fifteen years earlier, also died prematurely, an event that brought his black sheep father back to the fold for good after chasing after Marian Wilks.

Until then, the task of looking after Robert had fallen to Annie – rather unfairly, because although she likes him, she didn't see it as a job a not-too-mobile 70-year-old should have to undertake.

In 1990, Robert played the innkeeper in his school Nativity play. He invited Mary and Joseph into the inn because, as he said, where would Santa leave Baby Jesus's presents if they had nowhere to live? Some little while later, the police showed rather less charity to young Mark Hughes, who was booked while driving Robert to hospital after he was found drinking poisonous sheep dip.

Despite her misgivings, Sarah took Robert on when she moved in with Jack, and when children at school cast doubt upon his domestic situation in September 1992 he willingly granted Sarah the title of 'Mummy'.

And well she deserved it, having backed up her 'son' when Home Farm accused him of leaving a gate open between fields that let a pony, Shula, stray on to the road with fatal results. Robert's lessons on Treacle resumed when the blame was pinned on Holiday Village visitors.

Robert, who attends Connelton infants school, was delighted when in May 1994 his Mummy and Daddy 'learned their lesson' and tied the knot.

a surrogate mother, and finally accepted her as Mum.

The birth of their daughter Victoria Anne, named after the child's two grandmothers, in early 1994, seemed to set the seal on their relationship which had survived the collapse of the original Emmerdale farmhouse and financial problems that had beset the farming operation during the early-1990s depression. Though she hadn't seen herself as a farmer's wife, Sarah was finally married to Jack in May 1994, at the

JOE SUGDEN

The youngest of Annie and Jacob Sugden's three children, Joe, ran Emmerdale farm with brother-in-law Matt Skilbeck both before and after his father's death. It's ironic, then, that prodigal elder brother Jack should now be considered the farmer of the family, and it was his return to the farm in February 1980 that first inspired Joe to look for pastures new.

Looking locally, he joined NY Estates as farm manager in 1980 and went to France in 1983. He returned to Home Farm two years later to become NY's Regional Manager, reversing the roles with former boss Alan Turner. When NY pulled out in 1987, he and Turner joined forces to buy some of the estate, only to be pushed out by Denis Rigg in 1989. Joe then returned to the family farm – only to have history repeat itself when Jack came back from Italy once again after son Jackie's death.

Joe's marriage to Christine Sharp in 1974 was, sadly, little cause for celebration: it lasted just five weeks!

Joe and Kate Hughes became man and wife in 1989, but though events conspired to part them, he remained a devoted stepfather to her kids.

side were never going to make easy bedfellows – as Joe found when returning full of ideas from a fact-finding European trip to find Frank utterly disinterested. The writing was on the wall, and Joe quit after one final argument when he was 'caught' innocently entertaining the boss's estranged wife on his property, to wit the Holiday Village.

This was a less than fair reward for Joe's loyalty, particularly after the bang on the head he had received when Michael Feldmann, Steve Marshal and friends burgled Home Farm!

After planning a horse breeding operation with Kim once her divorce had gone through, he drifted back to helping out Jack on the farm – a state of affairs that clearly did not please him overmuch. And when his stepson Mark died in the Christmas 1993 air crash disaster he all but turned a shotgun on himself, which would surely have been the saddest of all ends to a life that promised much but achieved noticeably less.

His personal life was notably turbulent and encompassed two marriages. The first, in July 1974 to milk recorder Christine Sharp, lasted five weeks. Coming from a wealthy family, she couldn't adapt to the relative poverty of their situation, while Joe's pride prevented him from taking handouts from his father-in-law.

Numerous relationships followed over the years – most notably with Kathy Gimbel, the daughter of a local farmer, then with Barbara Peters, the married daughter of Donald Hinton who came to the village after the breakdown of her marriage. Joe and Barbara lived together and came close to a permanent relationship, but she refused to go with him when he was posted to France. (Barbara told Joe she was going back to her husband and told her father she wasn't.) Joe and Hotten Market auctioneer Karen Moore were also close for a while, but that was

The break-up of his second marriage and the employment of Michael Feldmann as full-time labourer left Joe in a state of limbo. He was rescued from this by Frank Tate in early 1992 when he was head-hunted to manage Tate's new Holiday Village. He even moved into Dolly Skilbeck's old flat at Home Farm, though Mark and Rachel stayed put.

But Tate's autocratic nature and Joe's stubborn

always doomed to failure as it followed Jack's marriage-rocking affair with Karen.

Then came Ruth Pennington, a local vet who ultimately couldn't decide between Joe and her fiancé, Liam, a wealthy Irish horse-breeder. Joe had better luck with second wife Kate Hughes, who turned up as Sandie's lodger, in 1988; they married in April the following year, but though he stood by her after the fatal accident for which she was jailed two years later, their future was always in doubt.

It was tragic that the baby the two had conceived was miscarried, for Joe made a reasonable fist of fatherhood – if only to two teenage stepchildren Mark and Rachel. And even though their mother quit the area for good in 1991 they elected to stay with their stepdad.

A capable, self-taught horseman, Joe taught Rachel to ride. He owns Saint, a thoroughbred bought for him by Ruth Pennington when his previous horse had to be put down after an accident. He was a keen sportsman in his youth, an enthusiastic fell runner and a stalwart of the local cricket team, and in October 1977 put this athleticism to good use when he joined the part-time voluntary fire service. He found immediate job satisfaction when he ran into former girlfriend Lesley Gibson, but as ever ended up alone.

Yet Joe's lonely life has had compensations. Living alone for so long – plus two years in France – made him quite a good cook, and he is capable of preparing an elaborate meal, much to the surprise of the occasional girlfriend like Lynn Whiteley.

His departure from Emmerdale in 1994 was understandable: he'd reached a dead end, both career-wise and personally, and suffered the death of his stepson Mark – for which he unreasonably blamed himself. While many were sorry to see him go, it is unlikely Emmerdale has seen the last of Joe Sugden.

PEGGY SUGDEN

When Jacob Sugden died, he'd intended his eldest son Jack to inherit the family business – even though Peggy, who'd lived on the farm all her life and who, with husband Matt and brother Joe, had kept it afloat without Jack's help, would have been happy to take on the responsibility. She was denied that, but when a limited company was formed at Henry Wilks's suggestion, Peggy, with her head for figures, was the natural choice for company secretary to Emmerdale Farm Limited.

Peggy Skilbeck (née Sugden) at Jacob's funeral. Tragically, she would die in an accident the following year.

In February 1973 she gave birth to twins, Sam and Sally – appropriately enough, just as the lambing season was about to start! Wilks, the newcomer turned benefactor, was chosen as godfather and took his duties very seriously.

Even before her happy event, Peggy felt she was getting under her mother's feet. Now she needed more space – and, as headstrong and determined as Annie herself, was not averse to saying so! Wilks again provided the answer: a smallholding known as Jamieson's he had included with the Emmerdale head lease when the limited company was formed. Despite talk of turning the farmhouse into a holiday cottage, Peggy claimed it, the Emmerdale directors agreed, and the Skilbeck family moved in.

But these were not to be happy times at Hawthorn Cottage, as the picturesque building was renamed. Peggy died there in her sleep in May when a small blood vessel burst in the brain. Dr Scott, the local GP, could do nothing.

Peggy was buried beside her father in St Mary's churchyard, just as the blossoms were falling. Matt, who inherited his wife's shareholding, found her loss hard to bear, turning his grief inwards for months and worrying Annie greatly in the process. After the further tragedy of losing their twins in a car accident, he took a second chance of happiness with Dolly Acaster, while Hawthorn Cottage itself is now the new farmhouse.

The Sugdens gathered in the Woolpack after the funeral of Jacob, in sombre mood. Peggy was later denied the inheritance of the family business, in favour of her elder brother, Jack.

The Skilbecks

MATT SKILBECK

QUIET, MILD-MANNERED farm labourer Matt Skilbeck proved a popular addition to the Sugden family when he married Annie and Jacob's only daughter, Peggy. Yet his life was soon rocked by the double tragedy of losing his wife and the twins, Sam and Sally, she'd borne him.

Peggy, who had expected Matt to be offered a share in Emmerdale Farm Ltd after Jacob's death, had been keen for Matt to leave farming and take a better-paid job in the town – something her mother scarcely approved of. As Annie remarked: 'You can't interfere between man and wife', but Matt was always happiest working the land.

The tragedy of Peggy's death in May 1973 left Matt – himself an orphan – the task of bringing up two small children while holding down a responsible job at the farm. That was clearly impossible: Matt knew, also, that two lively children under a year-old were more than his recently widowed Ma could handle with the farmhouse to run. The twins found a home at Blackfell with his Aunt Beattie, where they lived until a second tragedy struck, when her car was in collision with a train at a level crossing and they were killed.

A policeman flagged down Matt's car to break the tragic news, after which he spent the night stumbling around the moors, understandably numb with grief. A period of great uncertainty and distress followed: during it, Annie's strength of character as the matriarch of the family was apparent as she assumed the role of Matt's own mother in helping him survive a time of intense distress.

But time worked its healing miracles, and after false starts with Alison Gibbons who ran the village shop and Lucy Stubbs, a trainee agricultural worker at Hotten Market who briefly stayed at the farm, he found happiness with Dolly Acaster. When it came to choosing between between him and city slicker Richard Roper, a previous love who'd let her down, she opted for solid, dependable Matt.

Matt, Annie and godfather Henry Wilks celebrate the birth of the Skilbeck twins, 1973.

Dolly Skilbeck and son Sam form the charming centrepiece of this Emmerdale family gathering, at Christmas 1983.

Dolly, Matt and Sam present a pretty picture, one that was to fragment in the late Eighties.

For some time, the Skilbecks enjoyed a strong marriage which survived such strains as a miscarriage at nearly full term (though a son, Sam, was safely born in 1982) and an incident in 1986 when Matt was charged with the murder of petty crook and quarry owner Harry Mowlam. They'd been seen fighting beside the brook in which his body was found. Even though all the evidence pointed to an out-of-character act from the normally placid labourer, Dolly would have none of it. She stood by her man, and was vindicated when Derek Warner, a friend of Tom Merrick, confessed to the deed after an argument over the proceeds of a robbery.

Shortly afterwards, the Skilbecks were unexpectedly left a deserted farmhouse called Crossgill by an eccentric old farmer named Metcalfe. It was a ruin, but it was Dolly's potential dream home. Its destruction by fire after builder Phil Pearce left rags to burn inside the house was soon to be mirrored in the Skilbecks' own relationship.

Dolly's affair with timber expert Stephen Fuller devastated Matt. Even though he attended his rival's funeral in an attempt to mend fences after Fuller's accidental death, matters were too far gone.

Matt left in late 1989 to manage a new sheep farm near West Raynham, Norfolk. Frank Tate had set him up for the job, which he took because his problems with Dolly were coming to a head. She wanted a divorce and wanted Matt to take the blame for it, even though they both knew it was Dolly who had precipitated the break-up.

He had also been urged on by Teri, a young woman traveller, who had questioned his steady, boring and fruitless life at Emmerdale, making him question it too.

Safe, plodding, predictable Matt for once acted out of character and stole away into the night.

Not that he lacked guts: as leader of the rescue team, he went down the notorious Baker's Pot in 1977 to rescue a pair of trapped Scandinavian tourists. He was also the subject of a 1982 'transfer bid' when Alan Turner attempted to win his services for Home Farm by offering the old, recently vacated Tolley farmhouse. Loyal to the end, Matt opted to stay with the family firm.

DOLLY SKILBECK

Born Dolly Acaster in Darlington, the future Mrs Skilbeck wasn't from a farming background. She arrived in the village in 1977 to work in the Woolpack as part of a training scheme run by Ephraim Monk's brewery, and survived Amos Brearly's notable misogyny to become quite an attraction behind the bar.

She also became the object of Matt Skilbeck's affections after offering help when Annie fractured a wrist. But the course of true love was threatened when Dolly's former lover, Richard Roper, arrived on the scene. They had conceived a son when Dolly was still in her teens, and he had hopes of both winning her back and reclaiming their now-adopted offspring. After an unhappy Christmas weighing her future in the balance, she vowed to become a farm labourer's wife.

The wedding itself was a battle of wills between the bride's mother Phyllis Acaster and Amos Brearly – Dolly's self-appointed 'adopted' father – who moved heaven, earth and Mrs Acaster's recently acquired second husband, Leonard Purwick, to give the bride away. Dolly herself chose the dress of oyster silk, despite her mother's less than charming insistence that 'getting married in white would be dishonest'!

Above *Dolly's mother, Phyllis Acaster, was an overbearing presence in her daughter's life, particularly during Dolly's wedding to Matt Skilbeck.*

Left *Beckindale weddings are always traditional: here, Dolly is kissed for luck by the local sweep on her marriage to Matt.*

CERTIFICATE OF AN ADOPTION

Application Number **KC03**

(1) No. of entry	(2) Date and country of birth of child (see footnotes)	(3) Name and surname of child	(4) Sex of child	(5) Name and surname, address and occupation of a adopter or adopters	(6) Date of adoption order and description of court by which made	(7) Date of entry	(8) Signature of officer deputed by Register General to attest the entry
23724	Twenty-ninth October, 1967 England	Graham Peter Lodsworth	Male	William Steven Lodsworth 24 Birkenhead Drive Mansfield, Notts. (ex-army) and Mary Barbara Lodsworth, his wife of the same address.	Thirteenth March, 1968 West Yorkshire County Court	Twenty-first April 1968	James W Barnett

Adoption certificate issued by **JAMES W. BARNETT**   Registrar for the Parish of **HOTTEN**

James W. Barnett

Registrar of Births and Deaths

Sam Skilbeck was not Dolly's only child, as the village would discover in 1986 when Graham Lodsworth came calling.

Above *The birth of Sam in 1982 was an answer to prayer, and followed many anxious months.*

Right *Graham Lodsworth, Dolly's secret child from the late Sixties, came to find her in 1986.*

Dolly moved into the Emmerdale farmhouse from her vicarage lodgings after the ceremony, and was delighted when a two-bedroom extension cottage was built. But her dream remained a place of her own.

After the disappointment of a miscarriage at eight months which nearly cost her life in 1980, Dolly became the proud mother of a bonny baby boy, Samuel David, two years later. Sam the second was christened at St Mary's Church at the age of four and a half months. Motherhood suited Dolly – no-one but Matt suspected this was her second living child – but earlier events came back to haunt her at Christmas 1986 in the shape of Graham Lodsworth, her illegitimate son who'd deserted from the Army in an attempt to track down his natural mother.

The disappointment of losing Crossgill, her long-awaited new home, led Dolly into the arms of timber specialist Stephen Fuller, who was working at Home Farm. Though they went on a secret holiday together, she refused to run away with him and he was killed by a falling tree on the day she rejected him for a second time.

Dolly moved out with Sam (by now a pupil at Connelton Primary School) to live at the Mill, later taking a job as live-in housekeeper at Home Farm. She resigned in the summer of 1991 after Frank Tate had used her to get a contract from a wealthy industrialist. An ill-advised affair with councillor Charlie Aindow had ended shortly before she found she was expecting his child. After much heart-searching – and recalling her earlier miscarriage – she decided not to to go through with the pregnancy.

Dolly left the area soon afterwards, electing to try a fresh start just as she had some fourteen years earlier.

The Merricks

PAT MERRICK (SUGDEN)

BORN PAT HARKER in Beckindale, Pat Merrick returned to her roots in September 1980 after a disastrous marriage. She rediscovered romance with teenage sweetheart Jack Sugden, yet this happy event was to have unforeseen repercussions.

When Jack had left Emmerdale in the early 1970s after an argument with his father, he was blissfully unaware that his girlfriend, Pat Harker, was pregnant. Neither did Tom Merrick – the man who married Pat immediately afterwards while she was on the rebound from her teenage relationship was also ignorant of the fact. Pat had another child, Sandie, by Tom, and both were by her side when she returned.

After Pat's divorce, she became friendly with Jack again and they married at Hotten Registry Office in 1982 (though not until after a set-to between Jack and Tom outside the Woolpack!). By that time, Jack knew that Jackie was in fact his son, not Tom Merrick's. When the lad discovered the truth in a most unfortunate way, after an argument between the two, he was understandably resentful. Jackie had naturally regarded Tom as his father, and both took the news badly, but, by the time of Jackie's death in 1989, Jack and Jackie were close.

Ironically, Jack and Pat's marriage – the original catalyst for Jackie's rebellious outbursts – had been close to ending when Jack's affair with Hotten

The Merricks – teenagers Jackie and Sandie, plus harassed mother Pat – arrive in Beckindale, 1980.

CERTIFICATE OF BIRTH

Birth in the parish of __HOTTEN__

Columns:-	1	2	3	4	5	6	7	8	9	10*
No.	When and where born.	Name, if any.	Sex.	Name, and surname of father.	Name, surname, and maiden surname of mother.	Occupation of father.	Signature, description, and residence of informant.	When registered.	Signature of registrar.	Name entered after registration.
125	St. Margaret's Hospital, Skipdale	John Jacob Merrick	Boy	Thomas Merrick	Patricia Merrick formerly Harker	Farm Worker of Northcote Farm, Skipdale, Yorks	Thomas Merrick Father of Northcote Farm, Skipdale, Yorks	20 April 1964	James W. Barnett	

Birth Certificate issued by **JAMES W. BARNETT**   Registrar for the Parish of **HOTTEN**

James W. Barnett

Registrar of Births and Deaths

Jackie's birth certificate listed Tom Merrick as his natural father: only Pat knew the truth.

Market employee Karen Moore became public knowledge. A resentful Pat, wondering if her second marriage had been as big a mistake as her first, decided to act. Taking the bull by the horns, she confronted the lovers in their nest and laid down the law in typically straightforward style: 'Come home now or you'll never see me again.'

Jack had needed no second bidding, having finally realized where his responsibilities lay when Jackie was injured in a road accident. Tom Merrick was persuaded to look after Emmerdale while Jack and Pat kept joint vigil at their son's bedside. After several days hovering at the brink, Jackie finally opened his eyes and called Jack 'Dad'. Never before had he acknowledged him as his natural father.

Jack and Pat had a further son, Robert, in March, 1986, but Pat was killed later that same year when her car plunged down a hillside as she swerved to avoid a flock of straying sheep. By that time, she'd become part of the extended Emmerdale family, looking after Sam Pearson's vegetable garden and taking readily to life on the farm. Paradoxically, her death cemented Jackie's new-found relationship with Jack, and this helped both parties pull through.

JACKIE MERRICK

Jackie Merrick arrived in the village as a teenage schoolboy, and before long had found a Saturday job as assistant to gamekeeper Seth Armstrong.

Rebellion, perhaps predictably, followed his mother's rekindled romance: he consented, under protest, to live at Emmerdale after her marriage to Jack. However, after rowing with his real father Jack, one too many times, he moved back to the caravan his mother had earlier rented.

When he was sacked as assistant gamekeeper by Alan Turner (then managing Home Farm) for making a mess of a shoot for some important NY Estates clients, Jackie decided he would make a clean break and join the Parachute Regiment. Then he ruined it

Above *Even after settling down with Jack, Pat had to keep looking over her shoulder for her first husband.*

Right *Jackie learned much as assistant gamekeeper to Seth, including the fine art of ferreting.*

all by impulsively setting light to his NY-owned mobile home as revenge for his dismissal. Sentenced to community service, he went to live with Donald Hinton at the Vicarage, quit drinking and attempted to put some order into his young life.

Father and son were finally reconciled after Jackie was knocked down by Alan Turner's Land-Rover in an ill-lit country lane where he'd stopped his motorcycle. The multiple injuries he sustained put him on the danger list for several days.

Jackie's many romantic entanglements were the talk of the village: he even emerged from his five-month hospital stay with a new girlfriend, nurse Sita Sharma, to whom he was engaged for some while. After his discharge, he returned to Emmerdale to work as a farm labourer, taking a special interest in sheepdog training.

He found lasting romance with Kathy Bates, though theirs was initially an on-off affair. But he showed the strength of his feelings by smashing up the van of Tony Marchant, a short-lived rival for Kathy's affections, during one of several breaks in the courtship. Jackie also fell down a disused mineshaft in 1987 while looking for a missing, pregnant ewe – an experience that concentrated his mind long before Matt Skilbeck and the mountain rescue team discovered him.

Jackie and Kathy married in February 1988, living initially in the attic at Emmerdale before setting up a home of their own at 3 Demdyke Row in December, when Joe left to live with Kate Hughes. In the spring of the following year the couple announced that they were expecting, but Kathy miscarried.

The incident in which Jackie lost his life on 17 August 1989 was senseless in the extreme. He had

Jackie and the former Kathy Bates on their wedding day, the bride in Annie Sugden's wedding dress.

been hunting a fox that had threatened Alan Turner's game and local smallholders' poultry; Seth Armstrong wanted to dig it out, but Jackie struck a bet with his former mentor that he could shoot it first.

Catching the fox full in the headlights of his Land-rover, Jackie opened the door and reached for his shotgun. Tragically, he caught the trigger and fell, mortally wounded, to the ground, where Seth found him next morning. Jackie was buried alongside his mother, leaving Kathy a widow in her early twenties.

SANDIE MERRICK

Sandie Merrick was the talk of the village, while still in her teens. She was still a sixth former, and her relationship with the child's father, Andy Longthorn – the son of a local farmer and also still at school – was far from potentially permanent. Her mother Pat proved less than supportive, and it was left to Dolly Skilbeck – who, unknown to all but her husband, had once found herself in a similar situation – to fill the gap.

After much soul-searching, Sandie left for Aberdeen (where her father, Tom, was working on the oil rigs) to give birth, and subsequently had the ' child, a girl, adopted by a local family.

She returned in 1986 determined to make up for lost time, and became an assistant at Hotten Market. After getting rid of the dishonest Eric Pollard, who had originally dismissed her when she got wind of his tricks, she worked her way up to finally fulfil her potential and become manager.

Her personal life hardly ran as smoothly, however, and this was due in no small way to her affair with builder Phil Pearce. Their attempt to set up home together at Mill Cottage in Connelton in 1986 was undermined when he spent their intended deposit

Sandie Merrick and her daughter, Louise – returned to her when her adoptive mother died in 1989.

money. (She consequently kicked him out and took in lodgers to meet the bills.) She had earlier taken up with Terence Turner, the well-spoken but equally roguish son of Alan, but there was never any future in this either.

Sandie's life was then thrown into further disarray when a Mrs Fraser from Aberdeen contacted her. Daughter Louise's adoptive mother had died and the father had disappeared, so Mrs Fraser, the adoptive maternal grandmother, traced Sandie and got her to take the child back. Sandie returned to Aberdeen in May 1989 and now lives there with her father and daughter: Mill Cottage became the home of Chris and Kathy Tate.

The Turners

ALAN TURNER

WHEN ALAN TURNER originally came to the area in 1981 as a thrusting, if portly, mid-forties businessman, he was considerably different to the affable host who now resides behind the bar at the Woolpack. As manager for NY Estates, he ruled the roost at Home Farm, and soon established a reputation for being devious, lazy, and able to lay the blame for his mistakes at Joe Sugden's door.

The arrival of Caroline Bates after a succession of 'bimbo' secretaries was his salvation. He mellowed and became much less of a villain – a process hastened somewhat when Joe, wise to all Turner's tricks, returned from France to be appointed as his boss.

In his private life, Alan Turner was a lonely man

Alan Turner in thrusting businessman pose during his stint at Home Farm as manager for NY Estates.

with a failed marriage behind him. Terence, one of his two grown-up children, would reappear at intervals after being sent down from Oxford University. Turner Jr's unlikely schemes encompassed everything from 'home-made' lime pickle to a dry ski slope, while his charm worked on Sandie Merrick if not the other inhabitants of the village.

Turner Snr's relationship with Mrs Bates began as a need for professional survival and matured into a platonic friendship, which finally blossomed into romance after they slept together in spring 1989. They were to be married, and set a date for December – but the arrival of Caroline's mother drove a wedge between them and the wedding was called off by mutual consent.

When Mrs Bates returned for a holiday in late 1990 they went out for meals and found they still enjoyed each others' company, but too much water had flowed under the bridge for them to get back together. Not that this deterred him from proposing again in early 1993, not long before he met Shirley Foster for the first time.

Despite his apparent pomposity and self-righteousness, Turner could also turn on the charm. As well as Caroline Bates, he proved irresistible to a naturist called Rosemary, whom he met through a dating agency. (Confusing naturism with naturalism, Alan was surprised when Rosemary wanted to take off her clothes!)

His career with NY came to a standstill in 1989 when the estate was closed and he opted for life in the village rather than 'flying a desk' at NY's head office in Lincoln. The years between NY Estates pulling out of Home Farm and the Woolpack were filled by the fish and game farm, which Mrs Bates persuaded him to acquire. (Frank Tate took over the fish part in 1992, leaving Turner with the shooting rights.) It pitted Turner against arch-rival Seth

Terence Turner: expelled from Oxford and happy to ride roughshod over Beckindale's inhabitants.

Armstrong, but despite their backbiting he recognized Seth as a first-class gamekeeper on whom the survival of the business to a great extent depended.

Turner has a stallion, Champion, which he rode with the Demdale hunt but was more often seen driving his Land-Rover (having learned his lesson after a drink-driving ban in 1988). He enjoyed the

Vote for
ALAN TURNER
A Man you can Trust
In the Council election this Thursday
2nd May 1989

Independent by Name
Independent by Nature
Fighting for a Better Beckindale

status of councillor when he beat Kate Sugden in the local elections of May 1989, but soon realized he could make little real impression on Hotten District Council as an independent and let this lapse.

He found a much more suitable outlet for his talents in 1991 when he took over as landlord of the Woolpack when Amos Brearly called time after more than three decades. A natural gourmet, who fought a continuing battle with his waistline due to a fondness for fine food and wine, Turner decided to turn the taproom into a wine bar cum restaurant – an obvious outlet for the fish and game farm's produce. More important still, it also gave him the status of a pillar of the community.

But it still left him very much alone once 'time, gentlemen, please' had been called. He'd taken on Elizabeth Feldmann as book-keeper and administrator of the fish farm (after the retirement of her pregnant daughter Elsa), and had hopes of romance, but Eric Pollard won the day. Nor did tea dances prove to be the answer. The second Mrs Turner would not have been seen dead among the middle-class, middle-aged matrons at a tea dance; quite the opposite, in fact, since Shirley Foster had graduated to running a drop-in centre for destitute characters from walking the streets herself. (He and Caroline Bates had accidentally 'dropped in' themselves, assuming the building to be a restaurant.)

Having assiduously courted the enigmatic Ms Foster, whose principles and motivation both baffled and intrigued him, he took her revelations about her prostitute's past very well; indeed, he'd not long before travelled to Leeds with the idea of paying for a lady's favours in mind, but without the guts to go through with it.

Turner's political ambitions dwindled as he found respectability behind the bar of the Woolpack.

Former landlord Amos checks out his successor.

He refused to be deterred by Shirley's chequered past, and their marriage on 10 February 1994 was just what the village community, still shell-shocked after the air disaster of six weeks earlier, needed. Mindful of this, the bride-to-be had announced her acceptance of his proposal at a public meeting to discuss the setting up of a disaster trust fund, but the event itself was considerably more conventional. Samson the horse was pressed into service to pull the open carriage to the registry office, and for a few hours at least the still grief-stricken village was united in its joy. The future for the Turners was certain to produce fireworks behind the bar with two such strong-willed characters in harness.

And indeed this was so – until the siege of Emmerdale post office in June 1994 (in which Shirley was unwittingly involved when her Range Rover was hijacked) tragically ended the partnership. Selfless to the last, she interposed herself between Viv Windsor and the gun of her ex-husband Reg, ironically taking the bullet that had been intended for the one person in the village who had failed to warm to her outgoing personality.

Alan Turner and Shirley Foster's February 1994 wedding delighted the village community.

The Nelsons

CAROL & LORRAINE NELSON

ONE OF ALAN TURNER'S first moves on taking charge of the Woolpack was to employ a new barmaid after a succession of part-timers like Caroline Bates and Elizabeth Feldmann had proved unsatisfactory. Carol Nelson didn't exactly conform to the new, sophisticated image Turner had in mind, but there was little doubt that her presence would ensure the Woolpack remained the centre of village gossip for the foreseeable future.

While Carol was keen to discover others' secrets, there was much about her that remained unknown. When Jack Sugden suffered injuries in 1992 following an altercation with a pair of local youths, Carol brought her spiritual healing gifts into play, laying hands on him and immediately curing his disability.

She had been divorced from her husband for some time, and the arrival of their offspring Lorraine on the scene in the summer of 1992 caused grief to mother and daughter alike. The teenager seemed intent on falling into bad company: casual overtures of a romantic nature made to Mark Hughes and Archie Brooks led to rumour and gossip, after which she suddenly disappeared, sending her mother mad with worry. When she returned, at 2 a.m., Lorraine revealed that she had felt rejected since her parents' break-up and believed, wrongly, that she had been the cause of the split.

At around the same time, Carol was *persona non*

Mother and daughter, Carol and Lorraine Nelson, pictured in an all too rare moment of harmony.

*New barmaid, Carol,
makes the acquaintance of
her most regular customer,
Seth Armstrong, in 1991:
Bill Middleton looks on.*

grata at the Woolpack for a period after she
admitted making an anonymous allegation to social
services that Archie and Nick were negligent in their
upbringing of young Alice. Turner, the child's
godfather, dismissed her without debate while, with
the greatest of ironies, Lorraine was taken on as
assistant to Lynn Whiteley, who was running the
wine bar.

At length Lorraine ran away again, but on her
return contacted her one-time wine-bar boss with a
view to taking up residence at Whiteley's Farm.

While Carol immediately squealed her protests, it
became apparent that Lynn was to be the chosen
confidante for a horrifying story. Lorraine's father
Derek had, unknown to Carol, been molesting their
daughter repeatedly over the years. Having
discovered her father had a new relationship and
another daughter, Lorraine feared the same thing
might happen to the child, and to prevent this
possibility chose to reveal her ordeal. This she did to
Lynn: the subsequent revelation to Carol all but
broke her, at which Alan Turner offered the hand of

friendship and reinstated her behind the bar.

A combination of sympathy and therapy didn't stop Lorraine blackmailing Michael Feldmann, her fellow lodger at Whiteley's, when she observed him breaking bail. But a combination of time, love and tenderness (plus social worker Beth Anderson) finally did the trick and she returned home.

Lorraine had used her artistic talents to illustrate a local scandal sheet, compiled by Mark Hughes and then-girlfriend Debbie Buttershaw, which had been the talk of the village in the summer of 1993. Publication ceased abruptly after Shirley Foster and Alan Turner (the butt of many of the jokes) cooked up a spoof *Hotten Courier* story on the trio. This led to them breaking cover and enjoying a slap-up meal in the Woolpack wine bar, supposedly covered by the paper, before being advised that they'd been rumbled.

The rehabilitation of Lorraine continued apace when she was offered a job at Emmerdale Farm clearing the way for a farm shop. Along the way, she helped Robert Sugden nurse an injured barn owl, Olly. She taught Robert how to draw the wild birds of the district, as well as putting her artistic talents to use by designing a poster to advertise a trip to Blackpool organized by Seth in memory of his late wife Meg.

The arrival on the Woolpack scene of Shirley Foster certainly cramped Carol's style: was there *really* room for two dominant females behind the bar? The answer, unfortunately, was no – especially with Ms Nelson's holier-than-thou opinion of Ms Foster's chequered past, the expression of which was the possible source of countless rumours. And with Lorraine's acceptance at art college following two 'A' grades, the travel costs for mother and daughter were going to be prohibitive.

With untypical subtlety, Alan Turner managed to find an answer to both problems by persuading a

fellow licensed victualler to offer her a live-in job nearer her daughter's new place of study. So it was that the Nelsons disappeared into the sunset, little knowing the horrors they would be avoiding with the Christmas air crash just weeks away.

Lorraine's caricature impression of her mother's employer demonstrated a considerable talent.

The Tates

FRANK TATE

A PROUD SELF-MADE man who made a success of his haulage business in Skipdale, Frank Tate retired from the family firm in 1989 at the age of just 52 to hand over the reins to his son, Christopher. And, with a young wife and a country estate to enjoy, who could blame him?

His first wife, Jean, had died on Christmas Eve, 1984, after suffering for some time with cancer of the liver. Frank had helped her take a fatal overdose of painkillers, a fact he only admitted to his family six years later. It became public knowledge at 1990's Home Farm Hunt Ball, disgruntled ex-employee George Starkey having tried to use the information to blackmail him.

A family at peace, briefly at least. The Tates: Frank and second wife Kim, plus children Chris and Zoë.

Frank invites the Lady Mayor to open the Holiday Village, 1992. A happy Kim (in hat) looks on.

The news devastated Christopher and Zoë, Frank's daughter – particularly as it was clear Frank had already been having an affair with his secretary, Kim, who, fifteen months later, became his second wife. Yet the fact that Kim was also shocked by the revelations undermined Chris's initial accusation that they had conspired to kill his mother.

The sad fact was that Jean had supported Frank through the hard times, while he worked long hours to build up the business. She had put up with his drinking and it was only the affair with the much younger Kim, developing as Jean became ill, that made him change his lifestyle.

His purchase of Home Farm was further proof of that change in outlook, giving him the chance to settle in the country while leaving Christopher in charge of the haulage business. Another reason for buying Home Farm was so Kim could breed horses.

Shrewd deals since taking over the estate soon recovered the purchase price of around £1 million, but to Frank, the estate represented a chance to demonstrate how the countryside should *really* be run – hence his idea to open up a heritage farm to the public. The Holiday Village (opened with great ceremony in 1992) and health club were rather less countrified ventures, but Frank encourages Alan Turner's pheasant shoot if not always the local hunt.

Perhaps because of his guilt about Jean, Frank dotes on his kids, particularly Zoë. He had to be persuaded not to intervene when she dithered about finishing her university course – and, as subsequent events have proved, his patience was rewarded. His reaction in 1993 to her revelations about her sexuality was laudable, though his heavy-handed attempts to encourage a relationship between her and lecturer Jude Clayton were not as readily appreciated.

Christopher was a different kettle of fish. His questionable judgement has led many times to his being bailed out by his father, and with his mobility impaired in 1993 the relationship became even more difficult. Frank's genuine wish to help his son has never been readily understood, though the occasional gesture like the helicopter flight after his marriage to Kathy Merrick in 1991 was well meant and accepted as such.

Frank has fought a constant battle with the demon drink. In July 1990, he followed Kim and Zoë to her graduation ceremony in Edinburgh, but got drunk and failed to appear. Dolly Skilbeck, then Home Farm housekeeper, covered for him by telling Kim that his car has broken down on the way to Edinburgh and a grateful Frank promised not to touch alcohol again. A series of lapses followed, however, reaching a peak as Kim's infidelity became apparent.

Although not a fitness freak, Frank is extremely health conscious and – aside from his recurring drink problem – is well preserved for a man in his late fifties. He eats healthily and has been known to exercise, running round the estate and playing tennis on the hard court at Home Farm.

This stood him in good stead when encountering an old flame Ruth Jamieson, who'd visited the Holiday Village without knowing the identity of its owner. Frank was keen on rekindling the romance, but Ruth realized he was still hankering after a reunion with Kim and sensibly cooled the relationship before any harm was done.

Frank's heroics in the aftermath of the 1993 plane crash restored his standing both in the eyes of the community and his ex-wife Kim, though the tragedy also brought disablement for his son. Despite his wealth, he already knew that money cannot buy happiness, and he was also learning that drink could not wash away unhappiness. With his business ventures crucial to the village's financial well-being, it was to be hoped that the 'Squire of Emmerdale' would continue to steer a straight course.

KIM TATE

Frank Tate's former secretary never expected to end up Home Farm's lady of the manor, but no-one could accuse her of not enjoying the position to the full – despite the ups and downs their relationship has seen.

Her affair with Frank began as she helped run the company when he was caring for his dying wife Jean. They married in the spring of 1986, when Kim was 27 and Frank nearly 50. The difference in their ages has never bothered her quite as much as it has Frank.

In her own way, Kim is almost as tough as Frank, as she showed in their divorce proceedings in 1993. Like him, she also doesn't suffer fools gladly, as was shown when Dolly Skilbeck began to dither about taking the job of Home Farm housekeeper and finding sitters for son Sam: Kim told her bluntly to sort it out or forget the job. She was all for drastic action when Turner's stallion covered her thoroughbred mares and only cooled down slowly.

Kim realized early on that she was lucky to have a husband who could indulge her desire to breed thoroughbred horses, but also knew that she had to make a success of it, both for the sake of her own pride, and to prevent Frank either having to take it over himself or close it down.

Although she had always known Frank was unable to father any more children (he had had a vasectomy a decade before they met) Kim decided in the summer of 1990 that she wanted a child of her own. She persuaded Frank to undergo a vasectomy reversal operation, and was delighted in the summer of 1992 when she discovered she was pregnant. She chose to keep the news to herself, however, and it wasn't until she fell from her horse at the Hotten Show, breaking her leg and losing the baby in the process, that Frank learned the truth.

It was to be a devastating revelation, particularly since, feeling somewhat depressed, Kim was initially unwilling to try again. The coolness of their relationship opened the way for Neil Kincaid to make overtures, the result of which was their affair and Kim's expulsion from Home Farm on Christmas Day 1992.

Her subsequent determination to obtain a settlement that fully reflected her input to the Tates' partnership reflected a healthy self-esteem. In fact it was Kincaid's inability to recognize this that led to their affair being a short-lived one.

She had a (platonic) ally in Joe Sugden as she sought her independence, even living in a caravan as she built up new stables with the windfall from stepson Chris's purchase of her shares in Tate Haulage. But the fireball that engulfed Emmerdale on 30 December 1993 put an end to all that, as well as

Kim is a winner at point-to-point, but it was a riding accident that caused her to lose her child in 1992.

claiming the life of her beloved horse Dark Star.

Yet, as often happens, tragedy brought people together – and none more so than Kim and Frank. Her mobile home now a mass of smouldering embers, she was happy to move back into Home Farm on a temporary basis that soon became rather more permanent. Frank's leadership qualities, shown to the full in the aftermath of the crash, had reminded her why she'd fallen in love with this one-time captain of industry. And love was the one thing she'd consider putting aside independence for.

CHRISTOPHER TATE

Born in 1963, Christopher Tate has lived his adult life in the shadow of his father Frank, who worked his way up from one lorry to owning his own haulage contractors in Skipdale. Christopher's period as managing director of Tate Haulage was chequered, to say the least. Notably, his attempt in 1993 to gain outright control by buying his stepmother Kim's shares went dramatically wrong.

Chris Tate found it impossible to live up to his father's achievements as a haulage magnate.

He'd mortgaged his home to fund the exercise, and when his sister Zoë refused to back him with her shares in his power struggle he walked out of the company, sensing defeat. Yet he still found himself unable to escape his father's business umbrella, a brief spell as manager of the Holiday Village being followed by a Frank-funded attempt to follow in his father's successful footsteps and start a new haulage business with a single truck.

The Christmas 1993 air crash devastated many lives – but while time would heal most wounds, Chris lost the use of his legs through being trapped in the Woolpack wreckage and seemed likely to let this misfortune fester to life-threatening proportions. The only silver lining of the episode was wife Kathy's decision to stay with him rather than elope with suave American Josh Lewis.

Unlike his business life, Chris had enjoyed singular good fortune in his romance with the former Kathy Merrick. Indeed, he'd arguably been a good thing for her, persuading her to emerge from her shell after first husband Jackie died. He persuaded her to go out to dinner with him; she stood him up but he came back for more. A complex, intense character, Chris would not be deterred and despite arguments with her over her interest in the spirit world they became friends and, eventually, lovers.

He moved into Home Farm from his flat in Skipdale partly to be closer to her and immediately badgered her to move in with him. However, no-one was more surprised than Chris when she suddenly did so one day when he was working late.

Their subsequent life together, even after their 5 November 1991 wedding, saw many fireworks, since Chris was apt to revert to his bachelor ways – forgetting to tell her he'd be late home, and inviting long-term house guests like friend Alex. It took him

time to realize that constant care and attention, not the occasional extravagant gift, was the best policy.

His relationship with his father Frank has been both complex and tempestuous, not least because of his mother's death after a long and painful illness and Frank's long-concealed decision to end her suffering. Things got no easier when Frank made his secretary his second wife despite Kim being of similar age to his son. The possible conspiracy theories when Frank's involvement in Jean's death became public knowledge proved too much of a temptation for Chris, but after blazing away with wild accusations he eventually saw reason.

He gets on well with Zoë, but, like most brothers, could tease his sister most cruelly. He did not react well to her admission of being gay, and is fortunate that she has proved both stimulating and supportive in the aftermath of his confinement to a wheelchair. He could count on Frank's loyalty, but as ever had problems seeing Kathy's point of view.

ZOË TATE

After five years of study, Zoë Tate fulfilled one of her mother's final wishes and qualified to be a vet in the summer of 1990 at the age of just 22.

Earlier that year, it had looked as if she wouldn't stay the course, the prospect of working with male chauvinist farmers like Joe Sugden and Alan Turner proving less than attractive. That she went back to qualify was partly due to a common-sense chat with Jack Sugden, and also because of her success in identifying the *Cryptosporidium* outbreak at the Sugdens' farm, despite their initial objections.

She shares stepmother Kim's interest in horses, if not her riding ability, although she could ride sufficiently well to race Kim home from Skipdale when they had just arrived in the village. Until her

The love affair that never was: Archie's affection for Zoë could never be fully requited.

thought to the danger they faced. (Nick, in particular, emerged with a bad beating.)

In August 1990, Zoë got her first full-time job, with the veterinary practice of Bennetts in Hotten. In February 1991, she stepped into the breach and delivered Nick and Elsa's daughter Alice. Soon afterwards, she quit Bennetts, having become involved in the animal rights movement through her friendship with neighbourhood radical Archie Brooks. What she discovered about Bennetts' involvement in animal experiments sickened her, and she left both job and area that same year to take up a new post as a flying vet in New Zealand.

Returning to Home Farm at Christmas 1992, just in time to witness the collapse of her father's marriage, Archie once again showed an interest. Confused as to her feelings, Zoë – who had had boyfriends at university but no serious suitors in the village – invited him into her bedroom. Archie declined, recalling that Michael Feldmann had accepted a similar invitation and later been discarded.

It transpired that the confusion had not been over her affection for Archie but her own sexual orientation. She nearly took a job offer in Edinburgh, but when Archie offered to accompany her the idea was dropped and she found employment nearer home. And it was just as well, since it was her decision to side with her father and not her brother in the fight for Tate Haulage that helped being the family situation back to stability . . . of a sort.

Accepting her sexuality, Zoë made her peace with Archie and herself. But her first experiences of the Leeds gay scene – notably a poetry group where she met admirer Jude Clayton – were somewhat fraught and only time will tell how Zoë will adjust to the situation. She could, however, reflect on a better and more supportive relationship with her father than she'd ever known before.

father's marriage ran into difficulties she got on with Kim rather better than Chris did, treating her almost as the sister she could actually be.

Zoë has the intellectual power to contrast with Christopher's business brain and from the start got on well with his wife Kathy – even though their first conversations (for university research) were about the disease that cost Kathy her unborn baby.

A determined character, she recruited Nick, Rachel and Mark in a bid to stop illegal hare-coursing, leading by example, and giving little

The Bates'

CAROLINE BATES

THE MOTHER of Nick and Kathy, Caroline Bates was first seen in the village in 1984. Soon afterwards, she was appointed secretary to the then Home Farm supremo, Alan Turner, by his estranged wife Jill, who considered her far more suitable than the glamorous but unreliable types the wayward Turner tended to favour! With two teenage children to support, Caroline wasn't about to be driven out of a job she desperately needed by Turner's ever-changing moods . . .

Caroline Bates and Alan Turner explore York together. The pair came close to marriage in 1989, but they remain friends.

The two became partners in the fish and game farm, which she pushed him into setting up. Their relationship slid, almost despite itself, into romance, although in reality it was more of a firm friendship.

Caroline had split from her husband Malcolm due to his eye for younger women: indeed he married his second wife Sonia when she was in her early twenties – they have a son, William. Malcolm is now a lecturer at Hotten College of Technology.

As a mother, Caroline Bates was a much-needed steadying influence when Kathy first lost her baby and then its father, husband Jackie, in quick succession. Malcolm, by contrast, had always disliked Jackie, and Kathy rejected his clumsy offers of help.

Nick's unplanned parenthood with Elsa Feldmann also provided a challenge to Caroline, not least to her set ideas as to how children should be raised. However, she got behind her son and provided him with the support he needed to bring up Alice in her mother's absence.

In May 1989 her friendship with Alan Turner matured into a night of passion, and subsequently a planned wedding, with Henry Wilks nominated as best man. Sadly, these would remain just plans, as the bride-to-be left for Scarborough in October to live with her ageing, infirm mother, Alice Wood. She and Turner remained good friends, however, and there were even hints of a rekindled romance when he proposed marriage in spring 1993 before he settled down with second wife Shirley.

Caroline would return from time to time to keep an eagle eye on the prowess of her granddaughter, Alice – even though it took her time to get used to the idea of a male childminder, Archie Brooks, looking after her! In the custody battle that began in early

Caroline's mother, Alice, who lives in Scarborough.

1994 between Nick and Elsa, Caroline played a major role in the lives of both her son and granddaughter.

KATHY BATES

Born in 1967, Kathy Bates arrived in Emmerdale with her mother, Caroline, and brother, Nick, in 1985, following her parents' separation. She was then studying for 'A' levels, but left school when Alan Turner gave her a job at NY Estates as a farm worker. She was put in charge of the poultry unit at Home Farm, where thousands of battery hens were reared. Eventually, it became too much for her and she walked out – which didn't surprise Joe Sugden, who had advised against her appointment all along.

She worked part-time at Emmerdale Farm and in 1988 set up a farm shop with Dolly and helped make goat's cheese. Kathy was also a keen horsewoman and looked after Joe and Turner's horses. In 1989, when she and husband Jackie were having financial problems, he forced her to take a job at Hotten abattoir, which she hated: Jackie rescued her after a week.

Her relationship with Jackie lasted for several years before they finally decided to marry, his impulsive nature in marked contrast to Kathy's easy-going style. When they broke up during 1987, she went out with Tony Marchant, a rich relative of NY boss Christopher Meadows. This made Jackie so

Teenager Kathy Bates found part-time employment at Emmerdale in 1986.

jealous that he smashed up his van and pleaded with Kathy to go back with him. She agreed and they became engaged, marrying in February 1988.

The wedding was almost ruined when a burst water tank in the Bates' cottage destroyed Kathy's dress, the night before. The day was saved when Annie, Dolly and Caroline Bates altered Annie's own wedding dress – an Edwardian one worn by her own mother – which Kathy wore instead. Kathy and Jackie went on honeymoon to Tunisia and, despite unexpected adventures, enjoyed themselves.

The Merricks began married life in the attic at Emmerdale Farm and were delighted when Joe offered them Demdyke in December 1988. They were always struggling financially, however, on Jackie's meagre wage, supplemented by Kathy's earnings as part-time barmaid at the Woolpack. Her hours clashed with Jackie's so she gave it up.

Jackie's death, in August 1989, devastated Kathy.

After losing first husband Jackie in an accident, Kathy married into the Tate dynasty in 1991.

She took his job as a farm labourer at Emmerdale, as well as running their own 20 acres of rented land at Home Farm, until new landlord Frank Tate evicted her in January 1990. She was particularly involved with the sheep – both 40 of her own and 650 of Emmerdale's – despite miscarrying in 1989 due to the sheep-related disease *Chiamydiapsittaci*.

For several months she lost interest in everything, and only began to come out of her shell when she reluctantly joined the cast of the village play *Dracula* in January 1990. By this time, Chris Tate was keen, but she initially rejected his advances.

George Starkey, a lorry-driver who also tried to date her, brought news that a café owner in Southampton, who was also a medium, had a message from her dead husband. Kathy went to Southampton, despite much advice not to take such things seriously, but the inconclusive experience made her decide to get on with her life.

By this time, Chris Tate was becoming more important to her and their relationship flourished. In April, 1990, they spent the night together and in May, much to his surprise and delight, she moved in with him at Home Farm.

Any misgivings she may have had about doing this were heightened when Chris bought her a car after her old Citroën was written off by Rachel Hughes, to whom she was giving a driving lesson. Kathy's experiences had made her the more mature of the two, and Chris's belief that expensive gifts could solve differences would be the cause of many disagreements through their marriage.

Another present – this time, from father-in-law Frank – was their matrimonial home at Mill Cottage, though the couple eventually insisted on paying him for it. No matter how agreeable the surroundings, Kathy was never one for staying at home, much as Chris would have liked her to become a full-time cook, skivvy and bottle washer. A period of filling in as her husband's secretary saw her prove the point as she secretly gained her HGV licence, celebrating by backing a giant truck into a space outside the office as Chris looked on open-mouthed! She then went on to look after Kim's horses at Home Farm before the discovery of her boss's affair with Neil Kincaid put her in an impossible position and she quit.

She then took up her friend Lynn Whiteley's offer to help her run the wine bar at the Woolpack, but Chris was opposed to this – not least due to Lynn's oft-expressed low opinion of him. In 1993, Kathy's frustration with her husband's attitudes and activities would lead to a brief dalliance with hunky American wine rep Josh Lewis. She was on the point of eloping with him, but the discovery of Chris in the wreckage of the Woolpack brought her back to her 'senses', and, like the dutiful wife she felt she should be, Kathy prepared herself for life with a wheelchair-bound spouse in a purpose-built bungalow… organized, inevitably, by her father-in-law.
(As it transpired, they stayed put.)

NICK BATES

Like his sister Kathy, Nick, two years her junior, studied for his 'A' levels, but made a mess of them first time round. He returned to school to re-take them, but decided it was a waste of time and left – an episode that encapsulates his somewhat lackadaisical nature.

Since leaving school, much of Nick's life has been spent searching, often not *too* hard, for direction. He got a job at Hotten Market, working for Sandie Merrick, and showed considerable interest in making a career of it, but became disillusioned after Sandie left and the disagreeable Eric Pollard took over, so he packed in his job and went to France in 1989.

On his return, Nick began work as a gardener at Home Farm; though he only took the job – which he then knew nothing whatsoever about – because there was nothing else available. He has matured and now seems content with his daily lot.

If holding down a job until recently hasn't been easy, Nick's past romances have proved equally troublesome. His good friend Archie Brooks had lined him up with a girl on his eighteenth birthday, determined that Nick should 'celebrate his manhood'. Needless to say, he didn't.

He then became besotted with Claire Sutcliffe, a girl from Leeds who came to the area to stay in a caravan with her family. Observing a robbery at the village post office, Nick frightened off the robbers but saw the opportunity to pick up money they had dropped. He was hailed a hero until, much later, he confessed to his crime and received a suspended sentence.

In the meantime, he spent some of the money on Claire and asked her to keep the rest. She ran off to London with it and a broken-hearted Nick was comforted by her sister, Helen. She, in turn, became besotted with Nick…until he rejected her when she told Eric Pollard about his part in the robbery.

Pollard and Phil Pearce then blackmailed Nick into taking part in the theft of valuable fireplaces from Home Farm at Christmas 1988. At the last minute, Nick backed out and informed the police, but would prove a genuine hero four years later when he pulled Eric Pollard from the wreckage of his burning car after petty crook Steve Marshal had tampered with its brakes.

Claire Sutcliffe returned to Emmerdale in 1989 and she and Nick shared a house for a while. Nick finally lost his virginity before the revelation that Claire was married emerged, when her husband arrived in pursuit of her.

Nick's next love affair, with the assertive Elsa Feldmann, was rather different; the aftermath of this relationship made him grow up very rapidly indeed. After discovering Elsa to be pregnant in June 1990, he was keen to marry her and bring up the child – a display of previously unsuspected determination, possibly provoked by his own feelings of rejection when his father left his mother and had a 'replacement' son. It took some time to make Elsa believe he was serious and overcome her mother's opposition to her moving in with him, but this was an indication of the new, purposeful Nick Bates.

After leaving Demdyke cottage, Nick and Elsa moved in with Elizabeth Feldmann, but their intended marriage never took place, due to daughter Alice's unscheduled arrival. Although Elsa decided to leave both Nick and the village and took Alice with her at the end of 1991, she later returned the baby to its father.

As a single parent, Nick was assisted in raising Alice by Archie Brooks, who became her unofficial and later legally certified childminder. At one point, the arrival of a stepmother in the homely shape of Julie Bramhope, another single parent, seemed likely. Unfortunately, what started as a friendship ended as rather less than that when Barry, the father of Julie's child Rebecca, returned to the scene and she decided on a future with him rather than with Nick.

Elsa's return in 1993 was orchestrated by Elizabeth Feldmann who, up until that point, had proved a remarkably supportive grandparent to Alice and her father. Elizabeth's death that Christmas in the air disaster certainly didn't make the situation any easier for any of them, though Nick's employer, Frank Tate, was happy to offer moral and financial support to someone who he now regarded as a valued employee. Frank allowed Nick to live at Home Farm after Demdyke's destruction so as to

Above *Baby Alice was the fruit of a relationship between Nick Bates and Elsa Feldmann.*

provide Alice with the possibility of a stable home.

Frank's faith in his gardener was not surprising: as winner of the great village Marrow Contest in 1993 against such prize-winning growers as Amos and Seth, he clearly had the greenest of green fingers. Eventually, Nick won the legal battle for custody of Alice which had been ongoing since February 1994, but then had to cope with Elsa abducting Alice soon after with the intention of leaving the country. However, she returned Alice to Nick a short time later and the situation was resolved amicably much to the relief of everyone.

Opposite *Nick (foreground) is left at the Register Office on Valentine's Day 1991 as Elsa gives birth.*

The Hughes'

KATE HUGHES (SUGDEN)

Kate Hughes with second husband Joe Sugden and teenage children Rachel and Mark.

BORN KATHERINE HAMMOND in Sheffield in 1951, Kate married David Hughes in 1969 while still a teenager. They had two children, Rachel and Mark, but although they travelled widely around Britain and to Germany and Cyprus, Kate never adapted to service life, which her husband loved. If he had left the army while they were still married, they might have stayed together. As it was, the couple split in 1984 and were divorced in 1986. She remained fond of David until his determined efforts to break up her second marriage, to Joe Sugden, almost succeeded.

Kate moved to Hotten in August, 1988, following

a desire to live out in the country. This didn't suit her 'townie' children, but Kate decided she'd had enough of living for other people and wanted to please herself for once. She made her first home at the Mill in Connelton, as Sandie Merrick's lodger.

Kate first met her future husband Joe while a waitress at the Feathers restaurant, where he was dining with NY Estates' Denis Rigg. They then met in the supermarket, where Kate had a second job as a checkout girl. The pair argued on both occasions: Joe later shot her dog, which was worrying sheep, and from that moment it seemed they were destined to marry. Joe was the only guest to turn up to Kate's birthday party in October 1988 – and uninvited, at that! They started meeting in secret and Kate stayed at the farm for two weeks that Christmas while Mark and Rachel were with their father in Germany.

Soon after, despite opposition from the children, they all moved into Emmerdale Farm and the two were married in April 1989 at St Mary's Church. Donald Hinton at first refused to marry two divorcees. He eventually relented because it meant so much to them – particularly to Kate, whose first wedding service had been in a register office – though she and Joe were reluctant churchgoers both before and since.

After overcoming much difficulty, particularly with her son and ex-husband, 1990 began on an optimistic note for Kate when she fell pregnant, after initially being reluctant to tie herself down to bringing up another child. David disappeared from the scene after a final shotgun showdown with them, but her miscarriage in May was a major blow to Kate and Joe – and to Mark, who was convinced, wrongly, that his arrest for shoplifting was the cause.

Kate's first husband, David Hughes, was wedded to his army career, but belatedly tried to win her back.

Kate had given up her jobs at the supermarket and the Feathers soon after moving into Emmerdale and fitted into life on the farm very well. She liked to be considered a farmer rather than a farmer's wife and, up to her pregnancy, did all the farming jobs she could manage, including clearing rocks – by hand – from her two acres of organic land at Crossgill, where she grew kale (a cabbage-like vegetable). Despite her marriage, she remained fiercely independent and quite prepared to take issue with Joe, as she did when he and Matt made fun of organic farming.

A handy horserider, Kate also drove both her own Escort estate and farm vehicles though Joe wouldn't let her drive the combine harvester. She was quite happy to drink pints with Joe in the Woolpack, where she expected to be served with a man's glass.

Yet it was the combination of drinking and driving that led to tragedy in August 1990. Driving home from a night out with an old friend Fran, she knocked down and killed Pete Whiteley on the Robblesfield Road. Arrested and charged with death by reckless driving, she duly received a custodial sentence in October.

Having been released from prison, she told Joe in August 1991 that their marriage was finally over.

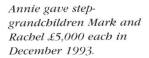

Annie gave step-grandchildren Mark and Rachel £5,000 each in December 1993.

MARK HUGHES

Born in November 1973, Mark was once considered the model son, until his troublesome teenage years coincided with his mother's relationship with Joe Sugden. Although he opted to remain in Emmerdale under the nominal control of his stepfather after Kate left both the marriage and the village, he remained prone to immature actions.

He ran away in January 1989 after discovering that his mother wanted them to live with Joe. He got as far as Hull, *en route* to to his father in Germany. Then David Hughes alerted Kate and he was brought home, but this was only after the entire village had searched the fells for him. He tried to get his parents back together on several occasions, and reacted badly to being clipped round the ear by Joe during the 1989 harvest for messing about with a gun.

In January 1990, he and some friends tried trapping mink with illegal and dangerous snares, but only succeeded in trapping Lucy the puppy. Being allowed in the pub with Rachel and older friends, he was desperate to prove his manhood by drinking alcohol. Again, he got into trouble.

He was then discovered, first by Rachel and then by Sarah, to be shoplifting, taking things he didn't need. His eventual arrest and warning at the police station was followed by his mother collapsing and having a miscarriage.

Mark obtained eight GCSE passes and, after initially expressing a desire to join the army in his father's footsteps, stayed on at school to study for 'A' levels in Art, Technical Drawing and English. But he reverted to type by refusing to turn up for his last exams - much to the disgust of girlfriend Melanie

Mark Hughes was an unruly teenager after his parents split, as this school report shows.

Hotten Comprehensive School

Annual Report of Achievement on MARK HUGHES
School Year 1991-92   Year 12

Art
Mark shows great promise, although impatience and inattention to detail has stopped him from getting better marks this year. He does not seem to realize that natural gifts by themselves are simply not enough, although his portfolio contains individual pieces of undoubted worth. Enjoys life class, but is apt to put his fellow pupils off with wisecracks and jokes.

Technical Drawing
Mark lacks the painstaking accuracy to make a real go of this subject. He tends to let his attention wander and make silly mistakes which could cost him dear in the forthcoming exams. To his credit, though, he has attempted to work on his shortcomings and is a pleasant, personable character. I wish him well.

English
Mark is one of our most able pupils, and has turned his attention to literature with great effect this year after a wayward first twelve months. His natural gift for language has stood him in good stead, and I am certain that if he does not freeze in his A-Level exams (his mock result was especially disappointing) he can attain a high grade.

General comments
Like his sister, Mark is well liked by all his fellow pupils, and looks set for a promising future if he can direct his energies into one last push for good exam grades.

A. Thomas

A Thomas, headteacher
Date: 16 May 1992

Mark leads the field in the April 1993 fell race, with (from left) Nick, Sangeeta, Jayesh and Rachel.

Clifford, whom he lost along with a promised place at Glasgow University.

It was the latest in a long line of problems and troubles. These had included letting his friends run up debts on telephone chatlines, a misfortune which led to him working at the Woolpack and neglecting his studies. (Annie eventually paid the bill once the extent of his folly was revealed.) He couldn't seem to hold down a job for long, working at the Holiday Village – where his job brought the 'perk' of a holiday romance with an older woman, Lisa – and as

assistant gamekeeper with Seth, until he got bored.

Despite his many shortcomings, Mark did have a sense of fun. It was this which led to him organizing events like the summer 1992 sheep race – run by lambs rejoicing in the names of Woolly Jumper, Red Ram and Mutton Jeff. He also arranged the following year's fell race, a challenge between the youth of the village (including Mark and new girlfriend Debbie Buttershaw) and sister Rachel's 'townie' friends from Leeds. Unfortunately, Lorraine Nelson was bribed to move the signs, and mountain rescue teams had to be called to search out the misdirected runners.

He got much closer to Joe over the years, and his stepfather was devastated when his insistence that the boy return a vacuum cleaner borrowed from Lynn Whiteley resulted in him being in the wrong place at the wrong time when a large section of the Eastern European airliner came down on Whiteley's farm. Mark was identified by the 1930s vintage watch his step-grandmother Annie had given him.

RACHEL HUGHES

Born two years and two months before her brother in September 1971, Rachel Hughes was understandably more mature than Mark in her reactions to the new situation the family found themselves in. Yet she was still hopeful that her mother and father would get back together, especially when David left the services with this in mind. She did, however, accept Kate's new relationship better than Mark, but as a vegetarian found life on the farm difficult to adapt to. At one stage, she attempted to sabotage Jackie Merrick and Pete Whiteley's veal rearing, which she believed to be cruel. She even used to drink soya milk, but now drinks cows' milk from the Emmerdale dairy.

As a schoolgirl, Rachel was friendly with Archie, Nick and Elsa Feldmann, who was in her year at school. The only boy from school she was seen with was a film buff called Andrew – whom she almost kissed in the Emmerdale hayloft during a conversation about D.H. Lawrence.

Her relationship with salesman Pete Whiteley began, almost innocently, over the summer of 1989 and consisted of little more than illicit meals and the

Rachel Hughes in 1994, the year she adopted a new, shorter hairstyle and put past events behind her.

THE GENERAL EXAMINING BOARD

GENERAL CERTIFICATE OF EDUCATION

This is to certify that
RACHEL HUGHES
born
16th SEPTEMBER 1971
sat for the General Certificate of Education at
HOTTEN COMPREHENSIVE
and achieved the result(s) indicated below in
JUNE 1990

ADVANCED LEVEL   (ONE SUBJECT, ONE PASS)
- - - - - - - - - - -

ENGLISH LITERATURE   GRADE A(a)

*   *   *   *   *   *   *   *   *   *   *

CENTRE No./CANDIDATE No. 3842 218   CERTIFICATE No. 291067

Signed on Behalf of The General Examining Board

C. E. Ramshatton

Secretary General to the Board

odd kiss, until Rachel's eighteenth birthday party, when she lost her virginity to him. Although meant to be the innocent, led on by a married man, Rachel actually seemed the dominant partner as the affair developed.

Yet it was the philandering Pete who ended the relationship when he felt it was getting out of hand, at the village bonfire party – just before his wife Lynn announced she was pregnant. At that time the affair was still a secret, but first David, then Kate got to know. Lynn, who had been suspicious, finally realized what had been happening at Dolly's New Year party. She later had a showdown with Rachel and the Whiteleys left the village for Birmingham soon afterwards. Rachel was not bothered, though she was far from proud of what she'd done.

The affair threatened her 'A' levels, and Joe and Kate were warned that her chances of reaching university were slim, but Rachel eventually worked hard on her English, Art and History and passed with flying colours to secure a place at nearby Leeds University, though she decided to take a year off before going and worked on a temporary basis for Tate Haulage.

Rachel took driving lessons from Joe and Sarah, having written off Kathy's ancient Citroën Dyane during her one lesson with her in May 1990. She passed her test two months later and now has an old Escort which takes her to Leeds and back.

When Pete Whiteley returned in September 1990, Rachel discovered that she had matured since their last meeting: she was now in control of both her emotions and their relationship. Although Pete's death upset her, she eventually rallied to her mother's cause. There has never been any love lost

Rachel's 'A' Level grades won her a place at Leeds University, but she put her degree course on hold for a year.

between her and Lynn Whiteley, however.

Rachel's rivalry with brother Mark reached a head when they transferred in early 1992 from the farmhouse (which Jack and Sarah were now to inhabit) to the farm cottage. Her subtle decoration schemes were countered by purple walls; horrified, she moved fiancé Michael Feldmann in to maintain order. When that relationship hit the rocks, she took up with young doctor Jayesh Parmar, the brother of flatmate Sangeeta. Yet a soft spot for Michael clearly remained, and after visiting him in gaol was won over after witnessing an act of heroism when he jumped into a river to rescue Robert Sugden. The pair were absent on holiday when the 1993 plane crash claimed the life of her brother and Michael's mother; she took the loss considerably better than he did.

In 1994 she cut her shoulder-length blonde hair into a severe short style, suggesting that a new, purposeful Rachel Hughes was coming into being. She was still only halfway through her university course, and despite occasionally helping out behind the Woolpack bar during vacations and working as a doctor's receptionist as she took time out to consider her future, Rachel seemed likely to pursue a high-flying future elsewhere.

A long-running relationship with Michael Feldmann brought Rachel both happiness and heartache.

HOTTEN COURIER

BECKINDALE EDITION

25 JUNE 1993

N. 95635

TEL. HOTTEN 3381

ESTABLISHED JUNE 21 1888

BECKINDALE MAN IN CAR CRASH MYSTERY
Foul Play Suspected, Say Police

Local businessman Eric Pollard was dragged from the blazing wreckage of his car yesterday after failing to negotiate a bend. The quick thinking of passer-by Nick Bates saved him, but not without cost to himself: the young gardener sustained burns to his hands which will keep him off work for some weeks to come. Mr Pollard was recovering in hospital at press time, his condition said to be 'satisfactory'.

HERO

Demdyke resident Bates, who looks after his young daughter, Alice, with the help of a resident childminder, was unavailable for comment. But his boss, Home Farm owner Frank Tate, was quick to commend his hero employee. 'Nick has always been one for acting first and thinking later,' he told the *Courier*, 'and on this occasion I'm very glad he did. He knows I'll keep his job open for as long as it takes - we're

BURGLARY

Meanwhile, speculation is rife as to the cause of the crash. Police who examined the burnt-out wreckage believe the car's brakes had been tampered with. They are actively seeking Steve Marshal, 20, whose part in a recent aggravated burglary at Home Farm was exposed by Mr Pollard. Ironically, the crash victim's stepson, Michael, was also involved in the robbery and was jailed along with Marshal: they are pictured below.

Anyone with any information on the crash or the whereabouts of Marshal is asked to call Sgt MacArthur at Hotten Police Station, telephone 27519.

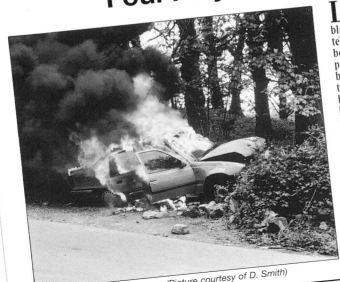

Scene of the blazing wreckage. (Picture courtesy of D. Smith)

things which happen during this situation, in control of

The Feldmanns

ELIZABETH FELDMANN

*I*F ANYONE deserved a happy-ever-after ending, it was surely Elizabeth Feldmann. Having brought up her children single-handedly after the death of her first husband, she'd learned to keep matters of the heart on the back burner. There'd been offers, of course – most notably from Alan Turner, her employer at the fish and game farm – but Elizabeth had been far too wise to mix business and pleasure, though she had to admit that she was flattered by such assiduous attention.

With Eric Pollard, it had hardly been love at first sight. His reputation as a shady dealer was well known, even to her, and she had few illusions as to what she was taking on – indeed, any she might have clung to were soon dispersed by her employer,

Left *Elizabeth Feldmann's wedding to local wide-boy Eric Pollard in 1992 did not meet with universal approval.*

Opposite *Eric's involvement in a car crash engineered by Steve Marshal earned him sympathy for a short-time.*

Michael Feldmann, pictured with mother Elizabeth in 1990, was the man of the family until Eric came along.

choose between her son or her lover – and Michael found himself as unwelcome at his mother's Demdyke cottage as he was in the pub.

Not that Eric Pollard was proving the ideal partner – far from it! Elizabeth was forced to lay down some strict house rules as Eric insinuated himself into her cosy domestic routine. Using her cottage as a repository for antiques 'diverted' from the auction room was beyond the pale, she decided, and to his credit Eric did his best to reform. No more would letters addressed to 'Emmerdale Antiques' appear on her doormat, and the path of true love – for the moment at least – ran smooth.

The union having been scheduled for a sunny early-autumn day in 1992, the appropriate traditions were set in motion. But while Elizabeth enjoyed a quiet evening with friends as her hen night, Eric held court in the Woolpack. Fortified by the effects of alcohol, he proceeded to disperse ill-judged insults among the surprisingly large number of males who were prepared to forget past disagreements and help him celebrate his last night as a free man.

The Sugden brothers proved to have the thickest skins, and took pity on the groom-to-be by laying him down in the pub's cellar to sleep it off. Unfortunately, he was locked in by an ignorant Alan Turner, and only a last-minute dash by Jack and Joe saved him from unwittingly leaving his bride at the altar!

Fortunately, all was well that ended well and the knot, at last, was tied . . . only for a police car to replace the usual waiting limousine at the church gates. Michael Feldmann's part in the Home Farm burglary had finally come to light, and he was led away, buttonhole bloom wilting, as the assembled guests hid their horror-struck faces and his mother turned the colour of her handsome suit.

It had been a day to remember, but for all the

Alan Turner, and Woolpack barmaid Carol, the fount of all malicious gossip. Yet such pressures seemed only to make her more determined to follow her chosen path: the Feldmanns had never had life easy, why should this be any different?

The main stumbling block, however, was son Michael. Used, for far too long, to being the only man in Elizabeth's life, he made no attempt to conceal his antipathy towards the interloper, Pollard, pressing the point home with a powerful right-hander of which Frank Bruno might justly have been proud, in the Woolpack bar. With this following hard on the heels of a public morality lecture delivered as the couple enjoyed a romantic meal *à deux* in the wine bar, Elizabeth was obliged to wrong reasons; and in retrospect it may well have been some kind of indication of the kind of married life the new Mrs Pollard could expect. Despite the ups and downs which followed, Elizabeth was to experience only a year with Eric Pollard – tragically, she became another victim of the air disaster of December 1993.

ELSA FELDMANN

Born in February 1972, Elsa lived at Keller Bottom Farm (the Feldmann family's 100-acre smallholding three miles outside the village) all her life until leaving for Leeds with daughter Alice in tow on Christmas Eve 1991. A classmate of Rachel Hughes, she left school at 16 to get a job, partly because of the continual struggle faced by her mother and brother in running the family farm. She wasn't able to find work until Alan Turner gave her a job on the YTS scheme.

A conscientious worker, she showed a natural ability with Turner's books, which is more than he did, proving herself a younger version of Mrs Bates by sorting out the mess that Turner habitually got himself into. She didn't mind working long, hard hours, partly because she enjoyed it and partly because she wanted to impress her employer enough for him to take her on permanently when the YTS scheme finished. Mainly employed in the office – at Turner's home in 27 Main Street – Elsa also worked at the fish farm, and as befits a farmer's daughter was not frightened of getting her hands dirty. Indeed, she worked hard at the family farm as well as for Turner.

Teenage mother Elsa Feldmann cradles baby Alice at her christening in the spring of 1991, watched by the child's father, Nick Bates.

Elsa's protective family background meant that contact with the opposite sex had been limited. She got close to Nick Bates, through meeting him with other youngsters in the Woolpack, but it took him a great deal of effort to ask her out and Elsa wasn't experienced enough to make it easy for him to do so. What was more, their dates were governed by an instruction from Elizabeth Feldmann for her daughter to be home by 9.30 p.m.!

When Kathy moved out of Demdyke, leaving Nick with the place to himself, he tried to persuade Elsa to stay the night. At first she refused and then, with Rachel agreeing to lie to her mother, she finally agreed. Nick left his contraceptives in the pub and their first night together resulted in Elsa becoming pregnant. Once over the initial shock, the Feldmanns decided to rally round, and Elsa and Nick moved into

Michael Feldmann and Lynn Whiteley had a brief fling in 1991, but Rachel Hughes remained his long-term love.

the Feldmann's farm (in separate beds!) in August 1990.

A marriage was arranged, but baby Alice was born on the very day – 14 February 1991, delivered in the Mill Cottage by vet Zoë Tate. Wedding plans were postponed indefinitely, and Elsa left Emmerdale at the end of the year, taking the child with her.

She later returned Alice to her father, being unwilling to be tied down in her early twenties, but in late 1993, at her mother's suggestion, started taking a more active interest in her offspring's welfare. This would result in a bitter custody struggle in which Elsa showed characteristic Feldmann stubbornness and an ability to stop at nothing that would have been envied by stepfather Eric Pollard; she even intimated that Nick and the late Archie Brooks were gay, in an attempt to strengthen her case.

MICHAEL FELDMANN

Born in 1966, Michael became the man of the Feldmann family at an early age after his father died. The farm he worked alongside his mother was poor quality land, fit mainly for rearing sheep, and finding their monthly rent of £350 was always a struggle. Although the living they got out of it was meagre, Michael was determined not to surrender to landlord Frank Tate who eventually evicted them. He was also proud and unwilling to seek help, and on one occasion sister Elsa had to call Jack in to help with a difficult calving.

Uncompromising and taciturn, Michael could be thought of by those who didn't know him as sullen. For some while, he preferred to drink in Hotten rather than in his local, the Woolpack, but rather than being deterred the local youngsters were fascinated by his brooding, independent nature.

Despite a one-night stand with Zoë Tate, his love life had been based around a relationship with Rachel Hughes, to whom he became engaged before she went to university in Leeds. Inevitably, the two grew apart and Michael was supplanted by Jayesh, the medical-student brother of a friend. With typical dogged determination, Michael refused to give up hope, and when he dived into the river to save Robert Sugden he guaranteed himself a renewed place in Rachel's affections.

Only her stepfather Joe Sugden questioned why Michael had been on hand to make the rescue: he had, in fact been following his ex-fiancée for some time, even travelling incognito to Leeds to observe her comings and goings.

Michael and Lynn Whiteley enjoyed a short relationship in 1991, but her interest in him was arguably spiced by his status as fiancé of her late husband's mistress. He later stayed with her while on bail, but in that instance, the domestic situation was always to be a temporary one.

His undisguised distaste for Frank Tate had made him a prime suspect in 1990 when an arson attack on Home Farm burned down a barn. (Jock McDonald was later revealed as the guilty party.) His feelings would fester and explode when, two years later, he was turned down for the tenancy of Winslow's Farm, a smallholding Tate wanted to turn into a heritage farm. Michael saw becoming a tenant farmer as a way to win back his (then) ex-fiancée Rachel. Frustrated beyond words, he became involved in the aggravated burglary at Home Farm which led to Joe Sugden being knocked unconscious and brought him a prison sentence. His arrest at his mother's wedding was an episode everyone would like to forget.

Having paid his debt to society, Michael was eventually taken under Seth's wing as assistant gamekeeper, but was victimized by the local police

West Yorkshire County Court
First Floor, City Hall
Leeds 16

Mrs Elizabeth Feldmann
Keller Bottom Farm
Nr Beckingdale
Yorkshire

Our ref: 069/RF2
Your ref: DC 020290

To the Occupier

Date: 2 November 1990

WARNING

A warrant has been issued against your premises. Together with this notice is enclosed the date and time when the possession is due.

You are required to remove all of your possessions and vacate the property before the stated time.

We regret that no extra time for accumulation of and/or removal of goods is allowed. If you are unable to remove all belongings, this must be in prior accordance with the plantives before the given day.

Bailiff

The Feldmanns' eviction from their farm by Home Farm newcomer Frank Tate rankled with Michael.

who, particularly after Sgt MacArthur's retirement, seemed keen to hang any petty crime they could around the neck of a 'known felon'. This, along with the village's natural antipathy towards someone who 'stole from his own', further fuelled Michael's resentment.

His mother's marriage to Eric Pollard – a man he both disliked and distrusted, not least because of his unwitting involvement in bringing the Home Farm burglars to book – and Elizabeth's subsequent death in the 1993 air crash, gave Michael two further chips on his shoulder. He fled the village in mid-1994 after attempting to murder Pollard, still unhappy and disturbed. It seemed unlikely he would return.

The Whiteleys

Lynn Whiteley pictured with son Peter, who was born on the day of his father's funeral in August 1990.

LYNN WHITELEY

MANY PEOPLE came out of the air crash disaster of December 1993 with their reputations enhanced; acts of heroism and selflessness were widespread, and the village managed to hold together where other, less closely-knit communities might have fallen apart.

Yet Lynn Whiteley, not for the first time, was the exception to the rule. Despite suffering the shocks of losing her husband in a road accident in 1990 and having her home destroyed in the air crash, she seemed unerringly able to rub people up the wrong way. In the latter case, she bedded the fast-talking tabloid reporter Gavin Watson, one of the least likeable of the newspapermen who flocked to the village in search of an 'angle'. After this, she was regarded by the villagefolk – not for the first time – as a viper in their midst.

Lynn had been a milk recorder when she married agricultural sales rep Pete Whiteley. News of his philandering with Rachel Hughes was not well received. Lynn, never the most trusting of wives (and with good reason), had harboured her suspicions, but only found out for sure about Pete's philandering at Dolly's New Year's party. A showdown with her rival was as inevitable as night follows day.

Once the feathers had flown, the Whiteleys had full and frank discussions about their future, which seemed, in Lynn's eyes, to lie as far away from the village as possible. When Lynn announced she was pregnant the Whiteleys packed their bags and departed for Birmingham in order to start afresh –

but Pete's inability to stay away from Rachel proved his undoing. His death was particularly ill-timed, Lynn giving birth to a son, Peter, on 28 August 1990, the day of Pete's funeral.

Lynn's subsequent return to the village, initially staying with father-in-law Bill Whiteley, was not universally popular; her man-hungry behaviour drew understandably disapproving responses from the village womenfolk. Lynn's advances to Michael Feldmann were successful, to Jack Sugden emphatically not. (When Jack's wife Sarah upbraided Lynn in the Woolpack, more than one woman present had cause to applaud.)

Business-wise, Lynn was a force to be reckoned with – not least because Pete's insurance policies and Bill's bequests (which included the cottage) had left her a wealthy widow indeed. She was not one to let sentiment stand in her way: a joint venture with Alan Turner (the Woolpack wine bar) was succeeded by an alliance with Frank Tate, the Holiday Village sports and social complex, which directly opposed her previous operation – much to Turner's discomfiture. In the wake of the air crash she staged a fund-raising night and, by engaging a troupe of male striptease artistes, the Nobbies, all but emptied the Woolpack.

Yet Lynn remained a sadly unfulfilled lady in terms of her personal life: in late 1993, she'd cast around for a prospective father to provide a sibling for only child Peter. She'd had a recent relationship with Joe Sugden, enjoying the revenge aspect of bedding the stepfather of her late husband's lover (until Rachel Hughes, the girl in question, emptied a gin and tonic over her in the Woolpack!) But even Jack wouldn't sign up as a potential sire.

No amount of commercial success could fill this

Though Lynn is shown here tending her late husband's grave, she showed considerable interest in others' spouses.

101

Pete and Lynn Whiteley, seen in a rare moment of marital bliss. Theirs was a volatile relationship.

Pete Whiteley made his first appearance as a friend of Jackie Merrick. A salesman by profession, he had appropriately been blessed with the gift of the gab – one he was apt to use on pretty girls as well as prospective customers of the agricultural supplies firm he worked for. Lynn, whom he married, was one of the former. They made their home at Whiteley's Farm, owned by his father Bill – a morbid character so obsessed by death that his conversation rendered people near-suicide.

The affair between Pete and schoolgirl Rachel began in August 1989. Initially, he was happy to enjoy Rachel's favours; it was a much-needed boost to the ego, and it did him good to feel the dominant partner in a relationship, given Lynn's ability to get her own way. But Rachel's physical commitment made their affair, in her eyes anyway, a whole lot more serious. Pete panicked, feeling things were getting out of hand, and ended the relationship at the village bonfire party in November. His timing had been perfect, because shortly afterwards Lynn announced she was expecting their first child.

Rachel managed to resume her 'A' level studies and gain the grades she needed for university, but Pete couldn't leave her alone. Drawn like a moth to a flame, he returned to the village in August, but found Rachel an altogether different proposition from the dizzy schoolgirl he'd bedded mere months before. She was now the dominant character, in control of both her emotions and the relationship.

One summer's evening they went for a drink – but Rachel, seeing Pete had been consuming rather too much alcohol (another Whiteley failing), confiscated his car keys. While making his unsteady way back to collect them, he was knocked down and killed by Kate, who was driving home along the Robblesfield Road after a night out with an old friend, Fran.

void. Despite signing up to buy Mill Cottage from Chris and Kathy Tate as a replacement home, the summer of 1994 saw Lynn leave the area intent on pursuing personal satisfaction.

PETE WHITELEY

The village has seen its share of bad boys over the years. Yet few have upset the apple-cart quite as dramatically as Pete Whiteley, the man whose amorous, adulterous designs on teenager Rachel Hughes ended abruptly when her mother Kate accidentally ran him down.

Pete's death devastated his father and wife. It also split the Hughes family in two: Kate was charged five days later with causing death by reckless driving. Nor would the story go away: a lurid account of Pete and Rachel's affair appeared in a Sunday tabloid the following month, scandalizing the village. Although life went on, Pete Whiteley still cast a shadow from beyond the grave.

Pete's once-illicit affair with teenage schoolgirl Rachel Hughes was soon the talk of the village.

BILL WHITELEY

Born in October 1918, just a fortnight before the end of the First World War, Bill Whiteley continued to live in his farmhouse after selling his land by auction in 1989. He had shaken hands on a deal with Alan Turner, but when Jackie Merrick got together a co-operative, backed by Emmerdale and Henry Wilks, to make a counter offer, Bill decided an auction was the fairest way of selling, and received £140,000.

Obsessed by death, Bill Whiteley's morbid and macabre sense of humour was a taste few were keen to acquire. His Christmas present to himself in 1989 was a coffin, because he felt he couldn't trust his family to spend money on a decent one after his demise. (He liked the idea so much he bought Archie Brooks one, too!)

He was friendly with Seth, but Amos and Wilks feared being left alone with him since his gloomy conversation could have them contemplating suicide after a few minutes – and Whiteley could, they suspected, suggest the best method. He only started drinking in the Woolpack in 1989 after Ernie Shuttleworth banned him from the Malt Shovel for his depressing effect on trade.

Bill was upset when his daughter-in-law and grandson left the shelter of his roof for Birmingham in 1989, and was understandably devastated the following summer when Pete was killed. Heartbroken, he died in July 1991, leaving Lynn and her young son the sole occupants of Whiteley's Farm, save for the occasional lodger. The farmhouse was destroyed in the December 1993 air crash; Mark Hughes (who was returning a borrowed vacuum cleaner) was the sole fatality.

Pictured here in 1989, Bill Whiteley had a morbid sense of humour which few in the village appreciated.

Seth & Archie

SETH ARMSTRONG

*B*EWHISKERED GAMEKEEPER Seth Armstrong was recruited to that position in 1978 by Trevor Thatcher, the first NY Home Farm estate manager, to prevent a glut of poaching – which Seth himself was responsible for! At this time, he was a school caretaker and had been taught to read while there by Anthony Moeketsi, a supply teacher from Uganda.

He quickly proved himself a skilled gamekeeper, using tried and tested methods such as a broody hen to hatch deserted pheasant eggs. Seth cares a great deal for wildlife and his knowledge is immense, having been nurtured throughout his life. He knows where to find badgers and hares, and the best ways to trap the predators that threaten his birds. He has little time for sentiment, though, and once shot a feral cat that Mark Hughes was trying to tame because it was killing his pheasants. As a gamekeeper, Seth hates the hunt: dogs and horses thundering through his coverts, only to cruelly kill a fox he could shoot far more humanely.

He has never had have much time for, or interest in, the fish farm, despite being obliged to work there. It was through the fish farm that he was affected by *Cryptosporidium* in January 1990 – an incident that confirmed his aversion to water.

He is more interested in river fish and has taught many of the youngsters how to tickle trout over the years. Jackie, Nick and Archie have all been taken under Seth's wing at various times and he has enjoyed their friendship.

Seth Armstrong seen in 1983 with his late wife, Meg.

Seth's marriage to Meg produced two sons, Fred and Jimmy, who have since grown up and moved away. Their home was at 6 Demdyke Row, on the end of the terrace.

He spends most dinner breaks and evenings in the Woolpack. His greatest pleasure in life is winding up the man behind the bar – once Amos Brearly, now Alan Turner – and there are numerous examples of his success. The Woolpack is his refuge, and he was not amused when Meg was once drafted into the pub to help keep Seth in order. She ended up bossing everyone around and the others for once appreciated what Seth had to put up with. Her death early in 1993 left him bereft, though he milked every last drop of sympathy from the villagers – notably Archie and Nick, whose hospitality he enjoyed to the fullest possible extent.

He can drive, but as a rule either walks or rides a bike. This bike has often been his downfall, as when it is outside the pub, poachers (once including Turner) know where he is…and so does his boss. When Frank Tate inadvertently reversed over the old boneshaker, Seth was bought a mountain bike, but was unhappy with it and successfully demanded a replacement 'sit-up-and-beg' model.

While a figure of fun to some, Seth is also capable of much common sense and hates to see someone in trouble. When Jock McDonald was going through the break-up of his marriage and turning to drink, it was Seth in particular who saved him from going under. He had strong words for Jock, though, when he got involved with the hare-coursers in May 1990, and this ended their friendship. Cowman Bill Middleton was another good friend.

The plane crash saw Seth temporarily homeless – but happy with a new canine companion, Charlie, to replace the long-serving Smokey.

A member of the local Allotments Association, Seth was not above cheating to win their competitions – though he met his match in 1993 in Nick Bates. He'd also employed subterfuge the previous year to avoid Turner finding out he had reached retirement age, but had to give best to Meg when she borrowed and used his newly acquired credit card before he'd had a chance to sign it.

Seth's constant companion, his dog Smokey, died in the air crash of 1993 – an end his master luckily escaped. Seth was absent, pursuing the widow of old friend Wally Eagleton with whose horse, Samson, he reappeared in the village after being presumed dead. This evocative image put Seth Armstrong on the front pages of the national newspapers. Even then, though, he ensured he was treated to luxury hotel accommodation and a long-awaited prostate operation at the newspaper's expense as the price of his co-operation. Seth's springer spaniel, Charlie, was also donated by the newspaper.

A man of many talents (his hitherto unsuspected piano-playing abilities rescued a Woolpack music night in 1994), Seth Armstrong remains as distinctive as his whiskers and woollen hat 'borrowed' from the wartime GI uniform. It was doubtful if even a woman as formidable as 'the widow Eggleton', who he moved in with in mid 1994, would be able to deviate him from his chosen path – from home to the Woolpack in as short a time as possible!

ARCHIE BROOKS

A resident of Hotten, where his mother still lives, Archie Brooks first gravitated towards the village as a friend of Jackie Merrick's through a band called the

A very young Archie Brooks, pictured prior to his childminding prime.

Giro-technics, but became more friendly with Nick Bates as Jackie and Kathy Bates got closer. Archie and Nick set off for France in 1989, but got no further than Leicester Forest services on the M1 – an episode that typified Archie's frequent inability to turn dreams into reality.

A capable mechanic, trained during a brief and unhappy period in the army as a teenager, Archie set himself up as village handyman in 1988 on a government enterprise scheme. Most of his work, however, turned out to be cleaning windows and the attraction soon palled.

He lived for a considerable time in a caravan, purchased by the villagers as a place to watch the nuclear dumpers on Pencross Fell. This was destroyed in 1988 by Nick in an accident with a tractor, and Archie consequently saw it as his right to move into the Bates' cottage. He also lodged for a while in the Woolpack before moving out to a barn on Kathy and Jackie's tenanted land. He shared this for a while, reluctantly, with the two goats from Emmerdale before disappearing in late 1989, heading for hibernation with his mother in Hotten.

Archie returned a teetotaller in the summer of 1990. He had high hopes of becoming a farrier, but could not overcome his fear of animals. He persuaded Nick to occupy Demdyke when Frank Tate bought it and he moved in with his old friend. Joe offered them £500 each to move out, and Archie needed little persuasion to take the bribe. He ended up lodging at Whiteley's farm.

Archie has espoused extreme left-wing views on occasions, but his talk of anarchy and revolution was rarely matched by actions. The youngsters regarded Archie as an amusing big brother but didn't take him too seriously. Most of the adults, particularly Amos and his successor, Alan Turner, actually liked him, even if they rarely showed it.

After trying an assortment of jobs, including grave-digging and truffle-hunting (both with Seth), he found his mission in life quite unexpectedly. Yet by taking on responsibility for the day-to-day care of Nick's little daughter, Alice, he put himself in the firing line with Lynn Whiteley who, as his then-landlady, had first call on his services. When she suggested a £20 per week rent payment, he moved in with Nick and Alice.

Archie's success with girls was patchy at best; prospects of romance hotted up in late 1992 when he double-dated Lindsay Carmichael, another childminder, with Nick and short-lived girlfriend Julie, but it came to little. The one great love of his life was Zoë Tate, for whom he'd always carried a torch. Zoë's discovery of her lesbianism in 1993 was a hard blow for Archie to absorb. Inevitably, he had felt rejected, hence his pub-crawl with Zoë's father which led to him driving when incapable, because Frank was even less capable. (Having foresworn strong drink in 1990, Archie had little tolerance for alcohol.)

Born on 30 November 1963, Archie Brooks had just turned 30 when he disappeared on the moors above Emmerdale. At the time of his death he'd been organizing fund-raising activities for Seth's much-delayed prostate operation, an activity that confirmed his spectacular rehabilitation from shiftless layabout to a pillar of the community. As such he is sadly missed.

Right *Two men and a baby: Archie, Nick Bates and Alice make a cosy domestic picture at Demdyke.*

The Black Sheep of Emmerdale

PHIL PEARCE

IF JOE SUGDEN ever had cause to rue the way his life has run, then he could look at schoolmate Phil Pearce and reflect that sticking to the straight and narrow isn't always a bad policy! Having left the Dales to find work in Brighton as a builder, Phil's return with wife and child in tow led to a number of unhappy incidents.

It wasn't long before Phil started seeing Sandie Merrick, who'd herself returned after giving up her daughter for adoption. Their affair was soon public knowledge – at least it was after the catfight that ensued when Lesley Pearce confronted Sandie in the Woolpack! The two set up home together at 3 Demdyke Row, with Joe as their live-in landlord.

Understandably, the arrangement didn't prove a happy one, and the pair started saving for a deposit to buy one of a pair of cottages at Connelton that Jack and Joe's company, Phoenix Developments, was converting from an old mill. Unfortunately the business hit hard times, and Phil couldn't keep his hands off the money – something Sandie only discovered when contracts were about to be exchanged.

Both business and love affair crumbled, and Pearce – at an understandably low ebb – was foolish

Phil Pearce, lover Sandie Merrick with golden retriever puppy before the duo's affair tarnished.

enough to fall in with Eric Pollard, whose unscrupulous dealings were in a higher league than his own. He began to fake antiques for the crooked auctioneer to sell, and when he and Pollard tried to steal fireplaces from Home Farm at Christmas 1988 there was only one person who was ever going to take the rap after reluctant accomplice Nick Bates pointed the finger. Since he had dealt only with Pearce, Nick could prove nothing against Pollard. Phil went down; Eric walked – end of story.

There could well have been a far more tragic tale to tell earlier that same year when Phil's negligence was responsible for the burning down of Crossgill, the cottage in which Matt and Dolly Skilbeck had hoped to rebuild their lives. By burning rags indoors Phil endangered the life of Annie Sugden, who was trapped by the flames. He made amends by dashing inside and rescuing the Sugden matriarch, but Matt and Dolly's marriage hit the skids some months later; adding, along with Sandie Merrick, wife Lesley and daughter Diane, to the lives he'd blighted.

ERIC POLLARD

Eric Pollard arrived as manager and auctioneer at Hotten Market in 1987, a man in his early forties whose past was something of a closed book. He immediately began to make life difficult for his young assistant, Sandie Merrick, and began a series of sharp practices like stealing antiques, knocking lots down cheap to friends and cooking the books. Sandie caught him and told Joe Sugden, who was responsible for the market as part of his NY Estates job. Pollard left under a cloud, later drunkenly confronting Sandie in the old mill and threatening her with violence.

Setting up as a private antique dealer, Pollard began putting work the way of Phil Pearce, Sandie's live-in lover, who made counterfeit antiques for Pollard to sell. Although his attempt to set Pearce up to steal fireplaces from Home Farm fell through, Eric managed to avoid being implicated and, when Hotten council purchased the market from NY Estates, returned to his old job in May 1989 when Sandie resigned as Market Manager. He soon made life intolerable for underling Nick Bates, who resigned.

The episode would, however, leave him in debt to Markets Committee Chairman Charlie Aindow, who was also his rival in romance: he succeeded in bedding Dolly Skilbeck where Eric's advances had been spurned.

But Pollard met his match when he fell for a con-woman called Debbie in the spring of 1990. As Market Manager, he was officially unable to own his own business, so gave her the money (several thousand pounds' worth of stock) to open an antique shop. Pollard had been in love with her and was heartbroken when she disappeared. The money he'd given her was borrowed from Charlie Aindow, who appeared on the scene to claim his debt and obliged Pollard to fiddle the auction accounts to repay the £2,000 loan.

He did nothing to endear himself to the village when he caught some of them stealing grain, which had been left in a field, in 1989, and then tried to steal it himself. They didn't believe his story that the grain was later taken away by the real owners, which was, for once, true.

Pollard considered himself a charmer but was disliked by almost everyone in the village: only Alan Turner showed him any sort of friendship. So it was a major surprise when he won the affections of Elizabeth Feldmann, who required convincing that his chicanery was at an end. He succeeded in this to a remarkable degree, even disposing of 'Sebastian', his beloved Triumph Spitfire sports car (though Elizabeth made him partially reimburse Mark Hughes, the buyer, when she heard the high price he'd negotiated from the unsuspecting teenager for a vehicle needing a fair amount of work).

Yet Eric's unscrupulousness was contagious, judging by Elizabeth's decision in 1993 not to disclose the find of a golden amulet on Frank Tate's land. This, however, paled in comparison with Pollard's tricks of paying Seth £20 for £500 worth of antique currency notes and stealing cheques from the fish farm chequebook and attempting to put stepson Michael in the frame.

It seemed that Michael was quite mad when, in the aftermath of his mother's death in the Emmerdale air crash disaster, he should claim Pollard was somehow responsible for Elizabeth's demise. Yet the arrival of his first wife claiming a share of the insurance payout on the grounds that he had conveniently forgotten to divorce her suggested that the Eric Pollard story was far from over . . .

CHARLIE AINDOW

Few characters have managed to make Eric Pollard look whiter than white – let alone inspire sympathy for him. But with his official status as Markets Committee Chairman allowing him access to Hotten Market's books, Councillor Charlie Aindow has always been in a position to call the roguish Pollard to account at any time. And as the man who reinstated Pollard two years after he'd been sacked from the job for dishonesty, Aindow's influence was far-reaching indeed.

A typical scheme plotted by Aindow and carried out by Pollard diverted valuable antiques offered to Hotten Market for auction to their own private clients at a higher price, the ill-gotten gains being split between them. While Eric vainly attempted to increase his share by fiddling the books still further, he was and remains easy prey for an operator of Aindow's expertise.

Bearded, and with an evil glint in his eye, Charlie was one of those characters who give local politics a bad name. Yet away from the political arena, his roguish charm has been known to prove popular with the female of the species. In 1991, he had a brief affair with the separated Dolly Skilbeck. Eric Pollard had already seen his advances rejected, and churlishly revealed his married rival's matrimonial status in an act of revenge . . . but to no avail. Dolly must have wished she'd listened, for on hearing she was pregnant Aindow abandoned her just when she needed him most. To add insult to injury, his only comment on her condition was an offer to pay half of the abortion fee!

Dolly's departure swiftly followed, but like a bad smell Charlie still lingered . . . and Frank Tate was to prove a willing adversary. Aindow harried the self-made businessman at every turn, attempting to block the approval of plans for Tate's Holiday Village in the summer of 1991 unless a substantial cash 'sweetener' was forthcoming, and threatening to close down his haulage business when it was discovered that the haulage business had a contract to transport horsemeat. While others raised ethical objections, Aindow was hot on the case wearing his public health hat . . . but once again was frustrated as Frank pulled a flanker.

Right *Councillor Charlie Aindow turns on the charm under candlelight as Dolly Skilbeck succumbs.*

Kim Tate and Neil Kincaid's hotel-room romps never translated into a stable relationship.

THE HON. NEIL KINCAID

The Honourable Neil Kincaid, master of foxhounds, proved a past master of mischief as far as the Tates' marriage was concerned.

The dashing stockbroker returned to the Dales at weekends to pursue his horse-riding interests and help his mother maintain the family seat. Yet despite his title, Kincaid's designs on Kim Tate were less than honourable. The loss of the baby she and Frank had wanted so much left her emotionally vulnerable – and Kincaid was cad enough to take advantage.

Kim found herself understandably attracted to a handsome man much closer to her own age than her husband and who shared her equine interests. The pair found themselves travelling to horse auctions together, and it was on one such occasion that the relationship was consummated. And though Kathy discovered the truth when she picked up a hotel bill the cocky Kincaid accidentally dropped while visiting Home Farm, the secret would remain safe until Christmas Day 1992, when Frank saw the expensive watch he'd fondly assumed was destined for *his* wrist being worn by his rival.

Neil was clearly delighted that Kim's expulsion led her to his door, but hardly as happy when Frank took the horse whip to him as the New Year's Day Hunt prepared for the off! Nevertheless, the bruised bachelor enjoyed having his wounds tended and hurt pride massaged.

His wariness of Frank faded with his injuries, and he was genuinely surprised to find himself staring down the muzzle of a shotgun when he and Kim tried to liberate her horse, Dark Star, from the Tates' stables. Frank's aim was diverted by daughter Zoë, but as the first shots were fired in a potentially messy divorce action, the cracks began to show in Kim and Neil's relationship. Kincaid couldn't see why Kim should fight for Frank's money when he could keep her in the style to which she'd become accustomed, while his mother and friends all made plain their disapproval of this mismatch of the classes.

The last straw came when Kincaid decided to acquire new stables for Kim to resume her business – without bothering to consult her first. There was a predictable clash of egos, and both parties resumed the single life. For Kim, it was a case of sadder and wiser, but Neil Kincaid seemed unlikely to change his died-in-the-wool ways.

JOSH LEWIS

They say opposites attract, but the man who replaced Chris Tate in wife Kathy's affections was in many respects a mirror image of her husband. Like Chris, hunky wine merchant Josh Lewis was blond and besuited; but where Tate Junior's charm soured in the bottle, Josh's refreshing personality proved just the pick-me-up Kathy needed when they met early in 1993.

His gentle ways and winning sense of humour brought the smile back to Kathy's all-too-often gloomy countenance. With the Woolpack's wine bar a regular stopping-off point as he plied the fruit of the vine to establishments east of the Pennines, the blue-eyed boy could afford take his time. And Annie's wedding reception saw the relationship show the signs of maturing into something altogether fruitier.

A rare tender moment for Josh Lewis and Kathy Tate in a romance that was ended by the air crash.

But Kathy was not going to rush into anything, even if she deserved more than to be saddled with an immature bully of a husband. That was to be Josh Lewis's undoing. Though he persisted in chasing perfectly petite Kathy, events conspired to dictate that he was destined never to be more than the shoulder she cried on.

When the air disaster struck, Josh was on his way to pick up Kathy. After finding his way blocked, he was instrumental in wading a river and helping repair a damaged bridge to allow the fire and ambulance services to reach the village. He gained the admiration of Frank Tate and many more besides – no mean feat for an 'outsider'. But as he followed the emergency vehicles into Emmerdale and saw Kathy holding the hand of her husband, lying pinned by a beam in the wreckage of the wine bar where Kathy had first met Chris's American rival, he knew their plan to run away together was doomed.

Returning to her cottage, he put her cases back in the wardrobe, removed her farewell note and, with a heavy heart, turned the nose of his car towards his next port of call – alone. In the end, Josh Lewis was just too nice a guy to win the girl.

The Newcomers

THE APPEARANCE of a new family in a small village like Emmerdale is guaranteed to set tongues wagging. The year of 1993 saw not one but two new arrivals – and in both cases they were to supply much-needed community services in the shape of the post office and surgery. Yet beneath their placid public faces, the Windsors and the McAllisters were as turbulent as any family with growing children . . .

THE McALLISTERS

It had been many years since the village had boasted its own doctor, so the arrival of Bernard McAllister and his family from their former hospital position in suburban Surrey was a cause of much pleasure. As luck would have it, the doctor would play a major role in the events surrounding the 1993 air crash and its aftermath, but the benefits of a surgery in the village – instead of having to travel to Hotten for medical attention – would clearly be felt for some while to come.

In all, Old Hall became home to four people: the doctor, his wife Angharad, plus teenage children Luke and Jessica. The position of teacher at local Hotten Comprehensive School initially gave Angharad McAllister the opportunity of keeping a motherly eye on her offspring – but the aftermath of the plane crash saw her lending a hand in non-academic ways as the school was commandeered for humanitarian purposes.

Once order was finally restored, the only thing

Bernard and Angharad McAllister were easily sold on country life; teenagers Jessica and Luke less so.

Left *Motorbike-mad Luke soon found like-minded company with which to roar about the Dales.*

Far Left *From boyfriend trouble to hogging the hot water, Jessica McAllister knows every teen trick.*

rending the peaceful country air was the noise from Luke's motorbike, which he employed to take him to his final years at school. He fell in with some dubious company, and his naivety seemed set to land him in some scrapes before he leaves to further his education, motorbike in tow.

Jessica, though two years younger than her brother, is rather more streetwise and can quite often prove more mature – though not in matters of the heart. Her parents had hoped a move to the Dales would put distance between her and 'fiancé', Danny, a long-haired youth some years older than her, who they regarded as undesirable. Like so many teenagers, however, Jessica proved less than willing to conform to her parents' wishes, and their disapproval probably prolonged the relationship beyond its natural end.

As may be expected given their positions in the community, Bernard and Angharad McAllister were soon well known and respected by all. They both played a part in the Turners' wedding preparations, and Bernard was a leading light in the administration of the Disaster Fund. Meanwhile, Angharad proved herself surprisingly uninhibited beneath a conventional exterior, most notably when persuaded on stage at Lynn Whiteley's benefit night to cavort with the semi-clad 'Nobbies'.

It was all a long way from their comfortable Surrey life, but for the McAllisters life in the Dales is just the prescription . . .

THE WINDSORS

Institutions like the pub, church and post office have been centres of village life for decades, if not centuries. The doors of Emmerdale's post office had remained closed for some while, obliging pensioners, mothers and the unemployed alike to travel to Hotten to collect their benefits – not to mention anyone wanting a humble stamp! So the arrival of the Windsor family to re-open the valuable village resource in the summer of 1993 was welcomed by all – even if Vic Windsor's Cockney wide-boy persona put a few locals' hackles up at first.

Vic had pooled his redundancy money – after being paid off from Ford's Dagenham factory – with the proceeds of wife Viv's late father's flat. Their intention was to get away from the East End overspill estate, where crime was rife and 10-year-old son Scott had already been led into temptation by street gangs, and re-settle somewhere the kids could grow up in a safe, healthy environment.

Vic and Viv each brought with them a child from their previous relationships: Vic's daughter Kelly, from his marriage to his teenage sweetheart who tragically died of cancer, and Viv's son Scott, brought up by Viv after she split from her ne'er-do-well ex-husband. (He was later imprisoned for murder.) Her parents, who disapproved of the match in the first place, disowned their daughter and grandson after the event. Donna, the Windsors' third child, was born one year after Vic and Viv married.

Only Vic has ever failed to doubt that their journey north was worthwhile. Scott was sceptical and ran away from home in late 1993 to revisit his East End roots, but Vic – alerted by Scott's Aunt Gina – persuaded him to return to rural pastures. Scott then fell into bad company at school: pressured to take his father's lovingly preserved Ford Zephyr on a joyride by schoolmate Glen, he ended up crashing it and was turned in to the police by his father. It had not been the luckiest of years for Scott, who, while accompanying assistant gamekeeper Michael

Right *Kelly, Donna, Viv, Vic and Scott Windsor pitch camp as they await the keys to their post office.*

Feldmann on his rounds, had been shot in the arm by poachers. The air crash hit him hardest of all the family, and he underwent a lengthy spell of therapy after being found drawing violent pictures.

Viv, meanwhile, took time putting down roots despite being three years older than her husband. Yet the post office offered her a challenge she was prepared to put her back into: she'd been a canteen supervisor at an engineering factory before falling pregnant with Scott, and was soon rediscovering her organizational talents and ability to work long hours.

Despite being the figurehead of the family, Vic was inclined to leave the shop-minding to his wife, preferring to restore old cars, motorbikes or anything else a budding handyman could turn his talents to. And while he could indulge a passion for rock'n'roll music, it was rare he found the time to take a day's fishing, his other pastime. Coming from a staunch trade union family, his brand of left-wing politics were unlikely to find favour in the Woolpack – especially behind the bar. Nevertheless, the hot-headed southerner survived his brushes with authority, like assaulting someone he caught looting the wreckage of the crashed airliner.

When Michael Feldmann let Donna Windsor ride on Emmerdale's tractor and promptly saw it topple over, the incident looked likely to end with a lawsuit, but when Vic later found Joe in a barn with a shotgun considering a quick but messy way out of his difficulties he relented and decided to let bygones be bygones. It was just as well Vic did, for Joe repaid the compliment in May 1994, freeing him after he fell into an icy Dales stream and was caught in underwater foliage. A raid on the post office by Viv's ex-husband in the same month saw it extensively damaged by fire, brought more bad memories for a family that had hoped to find peace and contentment in a quiet rural community.

Left *Scott, Kelly and Donna Windsor put a brave face on life far from the concrete jungle they had previously called home.*

Far left *Vic Windsor and his two loves: the old lady, Viv, and the old banger, a Ford Zephyr!*

The Disaster and After

A N EASTERN EUROPEAN airliner came down on the village on 30 December 1993 with disastrous results which were to affect the lives of many. Some survived, mentally or physically scarred, others did not. Veteran gamekeeper Seth Armstrong enjoyed a miraculous escape, and was feted in the press as 'the man who came back from the dead'. Archie Brooks, who shared his birthday with Seth but was some three decades younger, perished; his body, never found, was assumed to have been vaporised on impact.

Despite being lone wolves of a sort (Seth's marriage to his late wife Meg being one where each knew their place – his in the Woolpack, hers in the kitchen), Seth and Archie were both well-loved local characters. They enjoyed a strange bond as like-minded souls who felt themselves slightly apart from the mainstream. When the plane came down the Woolpack was staging a fund-raising night to raise cash for Seth's prostate operation – proof, as if any were needed, that the village community looks after its own.

There were others, too, whose names will always be spoken when the events of that terrible December night are recalled. The heroism of newcomer Vic Windsor as he struggled to save Kim Tate's horses as the flames engulfed the stables, and the decisiveness of Frank Tate as he cast aside the months of self-pity and liquor, co-ordinating the rescue operations and ensuring that a blocked bridge wouldn't stop rescue vehicles from reaching the scene.

There was heartbreak for Lynn Whiteley, who saw her house burn to the ground – thankfully without baby Peter inside – and joy for Elsa Feldmann when, against all the odds, baby Alice was freed from the wreckage of father Nick Bates's Demdyke home. She had already lost her mother, Elizabeth and could only cling to her brother as the rescue teams dug to successfully liberate the child.

While the Whiteleys had escaped serious injury, Mark Hughes, who had been returning a borrowed household appliance to their house, became the youngest victim of the disaster. Leonard Kempinski, who'd married Annie Sugden just months earlier, was the oldest victim: son-in-law Joe couldn't keep his car on the road as he drove the pair to the airport. As Mark Hughes' stepfather, Joe was to suffer twice over.

Some survived, but paid a terrible price. Annie Kempinski eventually emerged from her coma, but Chris Tate – discovered, ironically, amidst the wreckage of the Woolpack wine bar by his wife's lover Josh Lewis – lost the use of his legs despite the best efforts of Samson the horse to lift the debris that pinned him down. When gentleman Josh broke into Mill Cottage to remove the goodbye note Kathy had written for her stricken husband, he was arrested on suspicion of housebreaking, but Zoë Tate, guessing the truth, obtained his release.

There are memorials – in the Woolpack, the village church of St Mary's and elsewhere – of the events of December 1993 and their aftermath. Yet, if anything can be said to have pulled the village through, it is the spirit that made comrades of such an unlikely pair as Seth Armstrong and Archie Brooks.

THE DAILY GLOBE

PUBLISHED IN LEEDS

31 DECEMBER 1993

No 2,435

JET FALLS ON VILLAGE

'It came from nowhere', says survivor

THE sleepy Yorkshire village of Beckindale was today counting the cost of a disaster that came from the skies in the shape of an Eastern European airliner which plunged to the ground late on Thursday. Several local people are still missing, the confirmed death toll has reached double figures and it is certain that New Year celebrations in this remote area of the Yorkshire Dales will have been stopped in their tracks.

Beckindale ablaze in the destruction caused by the crashed airliner – the fires lasted for hours.

Devastation

Emergency services from the local Skipdale and Hotten stations attended the scene, but only after valiant efforts had been made by local businessman Frank Tate to create a through road where a bridge had been demolished by debris. Mr Tate, who declined to be interviewed, was today being hailed as one of the heroes of the hour.

A local woman, Lynn Whiteley, found her house burned to the ground, but though her child, Peter, survived unharmed, the body of a teenager was found in the burnt-out remains. Unconfirmed reports named the boy as Mark Hughes, stepson of local farmer Joe Sugden. Survivor Vic Windsor, who runs the village post office, was shocked at the speed at which the jet struck. 'It came from nowhere,' he said, still stunned. 'I just can't believe it. We moved here to get peace and quiet, and now this happens – it's like a bad dream.'

Cause

Cause of the crash is not yet known, but air-accident investigators flown up from Farnborough are presently sifting through the wreckage for clues. The black box flight recorder has not yet been found.

Tragedy

The Prime Minister has sent a personal message of sympathy to those who have lost friends and relatives, pledging cash

to rebuild the area. The only fortunate factor in this tragedy is that the jet descended on a relatively sparsely populated area of the Dales. The human cost of this tragedy has undoubtedly been high enough already, but if the plane had crashed on the nearby market town of Hotten, with 12,000 inhabitants, the death toll would certainly have been twenty times worse.

Epilogue

WHILE BECKINDALE – now Emmerdale – has seen much change in the past few decades, few could claim everything has been for the worse. The restoration of a post office, the establishment of a doctor's surgery – these are among the small, but important, improvements to the quality of life that have taken place only recently.

The task of the farmer, as elsewhere, has proved a thankless one with EC directives, the threat of so-called 'mad cow disease' or BSE, and ever-multiplying bureaucracy all combining to drive many to the brink of insanity. Indeed, Joe Sugden himself nearly became a suicide statistic in early 1994. Others, like his brother Jack, have swallowed their pride, turned a blind eye to past principles and embraced alternative forms of revenue-raising: in Jack's case, it meant going cap in hand to Frank Tate, whose methods he previously despised, to set up a farm shop in his holiday village.

Things were even worse for the Glover family, former tenant farmers who, in the summer of 1994, lost their livelihood when their landlords sold the farm for redevelopment as a golf course. Time alone would tell if Jan and Ned could exchange their caravan – won by Ned in a bare-knuckle fight – for something more permanent. But it seemed unlikely that any of their teenage children, Dave, Linda and Roy, would in future make a living off the land themselves.

When the farmers are having it hard, then the local economy invariably suffers. Takings at the Woolpack may not have been at their highest since the arrival of Alan Turner as host, but the village pub as ever remains the focal point for the locals – however much they are spending. If there's a spin-off from the tourist trade, then so much the better; but the Woolpack is serving hearty everyday fare these days, not the *cordon bleu* Turner had in mind when he created the wine bar, which is only common sense.

It was common sense, too, that enabled this close-knit country community to throw off the effects of not one but two cruel blows: the late-1993 air crash and the post office siege that followed soon after. Although individuals suffered grievously with loss of life and trauma, the community looked after its own. Outside media attention was not overly encouraged and the spirit that had seen the village through past troubles was once again rekindled.

So what picture will the Emmerdale family album show in ten, twenty, fifty years time? It's impossible to say, of course, but there seems little doubt that there will be a Sugden or two at the heart of matters. As modern communications make working in cities less crucial, it could well be that young people like Luke and Jessica McAllister will return to their home village after completing their education, setting up employment opportunities for other local people who otherwise might have to travel to Hotten, Skipdale or even Leeds.

It seems unlikely that farming will ever be replaced as the main means of employment, or that the Woolpack will be renamed the Silicon Chip – but it is certain that the challenges of the passing years will be met by the same determination and spirit of self-preservation that has kept this rural community buoyant over past centuries.

The Nineties will be seen as a watershed, if only for the change of name that followed the earth-shaking event of 1993. But Emmerdale life in the 21st century would, in many ways, follow the quiet, orderly and time-honoured patterns of years past, ebbing and flowing with the seasons and retaining at least some of the customs that have endured since pagan times.